Science Puzzles for Young Einsteins

by Helene Hovanec

Sterling Publishing Co., Inc.
New York

Contents

Puzzles 3

Specially designed for the science-inclined.

Answers 87

Confirm your work. Did you solve the problems...or not?

Index 96

Find answers to puzzles. Search out your favorites.

Edited by Claire Bazinet

4 6 8 10 9 7 5

Published by Sterling Publishing Co., Inc., 387 Park Avenue South, New York, N.Y. 10016
© 2000 by Helene Hovanec
Distributed in Canada by Sterling Publishing
C/o Canadian Manda Group, 165 Dufferin Street, Toronto, Ontario, Canada M6K 3H6
Distributed in Great Britain & Europe by Chris Lloyd at Orca Book Services, Stanley House, Fleets Lane, Poole BH15 3AJ England
Distributed in Australia by Capricorn Link (Australia) Pty Ltd., P.O. Box 704, Windsor, NSW 2756, Australia
Printed in Hong Kong
All rights reserved

Sterling ISBN 0-8069-3542-1

A to Z

Scientists are curious people. Some of the actions they might use are listed here. Put one letter into each blank space to make a word describing something scientists might do as they work. Cross off each letter after you use it, because it will only be used once.

A B C D E F G H I J K L M N O P Q R S T U V W X Y Z

E__ AMINE

__ UERY

__ EMAND

DISCO__ ER

INVESTI__ ATE

SEARC__

SEE__

Q __ IZ

INS__ ECT

TR__

SA__ PLE

RECOGNI__ E

__ TUDY

__ SK

O__ SERVE

S__ RUTINIZE

EXP__ AIN

__ NQUIRE

DE__ ERMINE

PR__ BE

__ UDGE

__ IGURE OUT

P__ OVE

V__ RIFY

U__ EARTH

REVIE__

Answer on page 87.

Criss-Crossing Trees

Place the name of each tree into the one spot where it will fit in the grid. Cross off each tree after you position it. One word has been filled in to get you going.

3 Letters
BAY
ELM
FIR
OAK

4 Letters
LIME
PEAR

5 Letters
APPLE
BEECH
CEDAR
ELDER
MAPLE
OLIVE
PECAN

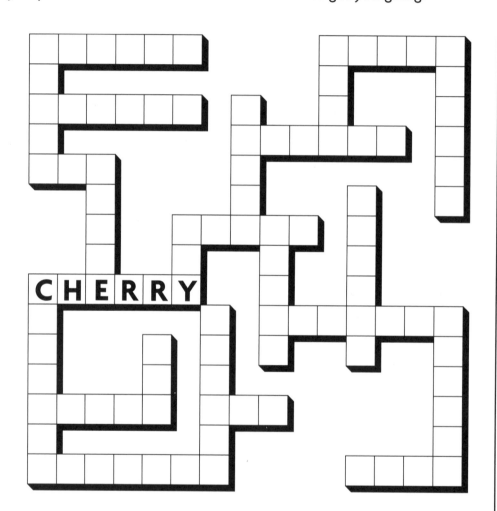

6 Letters
ALMOND
~~CHERRY~~
LAUREL   ORANGE   **7 Letters**
MIMOSA   POPLAR   AVOCADO
NUTMEG   QUINCE   CYPRESS
                      SEQUOIA

Answer on page 88.

Coded Riddle

Use this code to read a riddle and its answer. Write the words on the lines.

A = ■   H = !   M = ✦   R = &
C = @   I = ♣   N = #   S = ✪
D = %   K = ❖   O = ▼   T = ◆
E = ★   L = ✖   P = ❊   V = ●
G = $ W = ✔

✔ ! ★ & ★   % ▼   ✦ ■ & ◆ ♣ ■ # ✪   ✖ ★ ■ ● ★

_____

◆ ! ★ ♣ &   ✪ ❊ ■ @ ★ ✪ ! ♣ ❊ ✪ ?

_____

■ ◆   ❊ ■ & ❖ ♣ # $ ✦ ★ ◆ ★ ▼ & ✪.

_____

Answer on page 89.

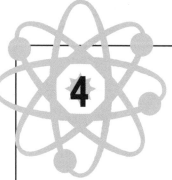

Science Study

4

Want to be a scientist? Here are some of the many sciences you can study. To find them, first figure out the answer to the clue in the parentheses ( ). Then write that word in the empty spaces on each line to find the science that studies the subject in the brackets [ ].

1. (piece of wood) B I O _ _ _ Y [living things]
2. (device for catching fish) E L E C T R O M A G _ _ _ I S M [electricity]
3. (sob) _ _ _ O G E N I C S [effects of very low temperatures]
4. (conclusion) D _ _ _ R O L O G Y [trees and woody plants]
5. (small rug) C L I _ _ _ O L O G Y [climates]
6. (cab) _ _ _ _ D E R M Y [preserving animals]
7. (not short) M E _ _ _ _ U R G Y [metals]
8. (curved doorway feature) _ _ _ _ A E O L O G Y [past cultures]
9. (steal from) _ _ _ O T I C S [self-controlled machines]
10. (Houston ballplayer) _ _ _ _ _ N O M Y [matter in outer space]
11. (family animal, for example) H E R _ _ _ O L O G Y [reptiles and amphibians]
12. (nickname for Thomas) A N A _ _ _ Y [body structure of plants and animals]
13. (light brown) B O _ _ _ Y [plants]
14. (ran into) _ _ _ E O R O L O G Y [weather]
15. (animal park) _ _ _ L O G Y [animals]

Answer on page 90.

Transplanted Body Parts

We've taken all the letters of some body part references and transplanted them into nonsense phrases. Each body part in the left column has a transplanted phrase in the right column. Can you match up all of them like we did for **STOMACH** and **HAM COTS**? Note: All the letters in the body part will be used in the transplant.

1. STOMACH **C**	**A.** CLEVER TIN
2. BLOODSTREAM ___	**B.** VEAL OIL
3. RIB CAGE ___	**C.** HAM COTS
4. TRACHEA ___	**D.** ME CURE BELL
5. DIAPHRAGM ___	**E.** LEOTARD MOBS
6. ESOPHAGUS ___	**F.** CARE HAT
7. SKELETON ___	**G.** BIG RACE
8. LIGAMENTS ___	**H.** MAC RUIN
9. SPINAL CORD ___	**I.** GRAPH MAID
10. CRANIUM ___	**J.** STING MEAL
11. CEREBELLUM ___	**K.** EEL KNOTS
12. VENTRICLE ___	**L.** COLD SPRAIN
13. ALVEOLI ___	**M.** HUGE SOAPS

Answer on page 91.

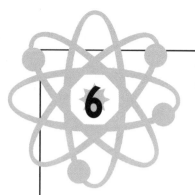

Constellation Find

There are 88 recognized constellations (clusters of stars). To find out the names of some of them, figure out the 3-letter word described by the clue in the parentheses ( ). Write that word in the blank spaces on each line.

1. __ __ __ R O M E D A (also)
2. __ __ __ T E S (scary word said on Halloween)
3. C A M E L O __ __ __ D A L I S (fixed golf score)
4. __ __ __ C E R (metal food container)
5. __ __ __ R I C O R N (hat)
6. __ __ __ I N A (automobile)
7. C __ __ __ A E L E O N (sandwich meat)
8. C __ __ __ E R (large rodent)
9. __ __ __ I N I (valuable stone)
10. __ __ __ S A (male adults)
11. M I C R O S __ __ __ I U M (police officer)
12. O C __ __ __ S (light brown color)
13. P E __ __ __ U S (fuel for automobiles)
14. P __ __ __ N I X (gardener's tool)
15. __ __ __ I T T A R I U S (droop)
16. S E R __ __ __ S (writing tool)

Answer on page 92.

Mini Fill-Ins #1

Complete each grid by putting the words into the spaces where they belong.

Fowl

CAPON
CHICKEN
DUCK
HEN
ROOSTER
TURKEY

Reptiles

CROCODILE
GECKO
IGUANA
LIZARD
TORTOISE
TURTLE

Fungi

MILDEW   TOADSTOOL
MOLD   TRUFFLE
MUSHROOM   YEAST

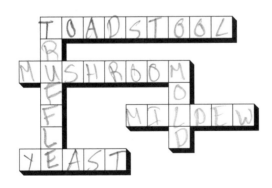

Cattle

BOVINE   DOGIE
BULL   HEIFER
CALF   STEER
COW

Answer on page 93.

Location, Location

Find an 8-letter word meaning a plant or animal that lives on a larger plant or animal. You can do this by locating the letters of this word, one by one. Read the clues, which describe exactly where each letter is located, and place those letters in the spaces that match the clue numbers.

1. Above "Y" and below "W"
2. Between "N" and "W"
3. To the right of "Z" and below "J"
4. Diagonally between "X" and "M" (look twice!)
5. Between "B" and "L" and above "M"
6. Below "V" and above "U"
7. Diagonally between "W" and "F" and "H" and "M"
8. Between "X" and "U" and next to "V"

F	Y	Z	B	S	L	B	F
D	X	W	V	M	Q	W	Z
G	J	K	T	V	N	P	Q
Z	R	H	O	F	H	Y	C
V	H	O	X	G	M	B	J
I	E	D	H	A	Z	Q	X
U	B	C	X	Q	M	V	E
B	N	A	W	K	D	M	U

Answer: __ __ __ __ __ __ __ __
       1   2   3   4   5   6   7   8

Answer on page 87.

The Machine Age

Write a letter in the blank space on each line to spell the name of a machine. Then read *down* the starred column to find the name of the science that deals with machines and the way people use them.

```
                    *
J A C K H A M M  E  R
         H A __  V E S T E R
              __  E N E R A T O R
     B U L L D __  Z E R
     T U R B I __  E
            C __  P I E R
          C O __  P R E S S O R
   T Y P E W R __  T E R
              __  O M P U T E R
        F A C __  I M I L E
```

Answer on page 88.

10 For the Birds

Find and circle the names of 27 birds in the grid below. Look across, up, down, and diagonally, both forward and backward. **CONDOR** has been circled to start you off. After you've found and circled all the words, put the leftover letters into the blank spaces below. Keep the letters in order, from left to right and top to bottom, and you'll answer this riddle: What do you call a bird who tattles to a lifeguard?

CANARY
CARDINAL
CONDOR
CROW
DODO
DOVE
EAGLE
FALCON
FINCH
GOOSE
GULL
HERON
JAY
KIWI
LARK
LOON
MALLARD
ORIOLE
PELICAN
RAVEN
ROBIN

A	H	C	N	I	F	P	O	W	D	C
D	R	A	L	L	A	M	O	O	A	O
E	S	O	O	G	L	R	D	R	J	N
P	S	L	B	O	C	O	D	L	A	D
E	W	L	W	I	O	I	O	P	Y	O
L	A	U	O	I	N	K	S	N	R	R
I	N	G	L	A	D	R	T	I	A	A
C	O	T	L	G	O	A	O	K	N	V
A	R	E	A	E	V	L	R	I	A	E
N	E	R	W	E	E	O	K	W	C	N
N	H	N	S	T	A	R	L	I	N	G

STARLING   SWALLOW   TERN
STORK   SWAN   WREN

Riddle answer: __ _____ _____

Answer on page 89.

12

Close Relatives #1

Change one letter in each word to find three words that belong together in each group. Write the new words on the lines. The first one is done for you

1. Dogs
FIX MERRIER **FOX TERRIER**
TREAT LANE _____
DRENCH NOODLE _____

2. Insects
MELLOW PACKET _____
COACH _____
WAFER MUG _____

3. Fish
CROOK GROUT _____
SLING ROY _____
BLOCK TEA LASS _____

4. Amphibians
FLOG _____
GOAD _____
NEWS _____

5. Healthy Foods
OAR GRAN _____
WHALE CHEAT DREAD _____
SKIP SILK _____

6. Junk Foods
DREAM CUFF _____
DANDY _____
WRENCH FLIES _____

7. Mammals
MILD BOAT _____
MOLAR HEAR _____
GLUE BOX _____

8. Baby Animals
THICK _____
HALF _____
FOOL _____

9. Forest Workers
MARK DANGER _____
JOGGER _____
GOOD SHOPPER _____

10. Plant Parts
STEW _____
LEAD _____
BOOT _____

11. Birds
LOVE _____
GAWK _____
CARROT _____

12. Precipitation
FLEET _____
SHOW _____
WAIL _____

13. Metals
BOLD _____
SOLVER _____
HOPPER _____

14. Snakes
ODDER _____
WIPER _____
TATTLER _____

Answer on page 91.

Eye Cue

12

Add one letter to each line to make two new words. The added letter will be the end of the word on the left and the beginning of the word on the right. Example: Put **O** on the first line to make **CELLO** and **OPEN**, as we did. When you're done, read *down* the column to find someone who is an eye specialist. Make sure that the letters you add work for both words!

CELL	**O**	PEN
TRAM	__	RICE
PLUS	__	AIR
CHAR	__	RAIL
FORT	__	ILL
SAG	__	WAKE
EASE	__	ADDER
SPAS	__	OTHER
RODE	__	WING
GAVE	__	EVER
PINT	__	PAL
THIN	__	HOST
SWAM	__	CON
DISCUS	__	PRINT
FINES	__	RAVEL

Answer on page 92.

Cute Critter

Change each letter below to the one that comes *immediately* before it in the alphabet (example: change every **B** to an **A**) and you'll find a piece of information about a critter you probably never heard about. Write the new words on the lines.

B   X B U F S   C F B S   J T   B   U J O Z

_____

D S F B U V S F   O P   C J H H F S   U I B O

_____

P O F   H S B J O   P G   T B O E .   X J F O   J U

_____

D B O O P U   G J O E   X B U F S   J U

_____

T U P Q T   F B U J O H ,   N P W J O H ,   B O E

_____

C S F B U J O H ,   B O E   T F F N T   U P   C F

_____

E F B E .   C V U   X I F O   T D J F O U J T U T

_____

B E E   X B U F S   U P   J U ,   U I F   U J O Z

_____

B O J N B M   D P N F T   C B D L   U P   M J G F .

_____

Answer on page 93.

14 Cold Stuff

Figure out the word that completes each sentence and find it in the same numbered row in the diagram. Cross out the word, letter by letter. All the letters of an answer will always be next to each other, but there will be extra letters on each line. When you're finished, put these *leftover* letters in the spaces below. Work from left to right and top to bottom, and you'll find the name of a very cold place.

1. Water that has been made solid by the cold is ___ .
1. The ___ is the coldest part of the refrigerator.
2. Black-and-white sea birds that live in cold places are called ___ .
3. A ___ is a huge mass of ice that has formed over many years.
3. ___ is a form of winter precipitation.
4. It can get very cold in the state of ___ .
4. Many people enjoy skiing, in the Swiss ___ .
5. ___ have flippers and live in cold ocean waters.
5. Large pieces of floating ice are called ___ .
6. The area at one end of the Earth is the ___ ___ .
7. ___ are very large mammals that look like fish . . .
7. . . . and the main food that they eat is called ___ .

1	I	C	E	C	F	R	E	E	Z	E	R	O
2	N	P	E	N	G	U	I	N	S	T	I	N
3	G	L	A	C	I	E	R	E	S	N	O	W
4	A	L	A	S	K	A	N	T	A	L	P	S
5	S	E	A	L	S	O	F	L	O	E	S	F
6	S	O	U	T	H	P	O	L	E	A	N	T
7	A	W	H	A	L	E	S	K	R	I	L	L
8	C	R	E	V	A	S	S	E	S	R	C	T
9	I	C	S	A	T	E	L	L	I	T	E	S
10	B	L	U	E	A	B	L	U	B	B	E	R

8. Deep cracks in the row **3** items are called ___ .
9. ___ are bodies that circle the earth and give weather information.
10. When you're very cold you might turn ___ .
10. ___ is the fat of row **5** and **7** mammals.

Answer:

— — — — — — — — —
— —
— — — — — — — — — — — .

Answer on page 94.

Going Batty

There's a BAT on each line below and it's part of a longer word. Just fill in the blanks with letters to form words that answer the clues in the parentheses ( ) and you'll be completely BATty!

1. __ __ __ __ B A T (a person who is good at physical stunts)
2. B A T __ __ __ __ (groups of cookies)
3. B A T __ __ __ __ __ (what you wear after a shower)
4. B A T __ __ __ (Robin's friend who wears a cape)
5. B A T __ __ (what a twirler twirls)
6. B A T __ __ __ (what a cake is before it's baked)
7. B A T __ __ __ __ (source of energy for a Walkman)
8. B A T __ __ __ (a fight)
9. B A T __ __ __ __ __ __ __ (a war boat)
10. __ __ B A T __ (a verbal contest or discussion)
11. __ __ __ __ B A T __ __ (a place where a baby chick is hatched)
12. __ __ __ B A T __ __ __ __ (people who tan themselves at the beach)
13. __ __ B A T __ (a refund)
14. __ __ __ B A T __ (a day set aside for worship)

Answer on page 87.

Cross-Offs

16

Cross off the words described below. Then read the *remaining* words from *right to left* and *bottom to top* to find the answer to this riddle: What happens to grapes that are under a lot of stress?

Cross off:

a. 3 rodents

b. 4 words that start with "W" and end with "N"

c. 3 planets

d. 4 meats

e. 2 synonyms for youngsters

f. 4 zoo animals

g. 3 Olympic medals

h. 3 words that contain only the letters **A**, **C**, **E**, and **R**

i. 3 types of pasta

j. 3 time words

k. 4 bodies of water

TOMORROW   RAISINS   LIVER   WAN   MOLE   WOVEN

LAGOON   YESTERDAY   INTO   BABIES   URANUS

STEAK   CARE   PANTHER   VEAL   TODAY   TURN

PLUTO   MOUSE   TIGER   MACARONI   ACRE   AND

PORK   POND   WIN   RACE   ZITI   TODDLERS   ZEBRA

LION   WRINKLED   SILVER   WHEN   BRONZE   RAT

GET   SEA   GOLD   SPAGHETTI   THEY   VENUS   LAKE

Answer on page 89.

Intersecting Numbers

In the grid below some letters of the alphabet meet at the intersection of 2 numbers, one in the Across row and one in the Down column. Example: the letter **A** meets at the intersection of **1** in the Down column and **7** in the Across row. Change each intersection point to the letter it represents to read a riddle and its answer. Write the letters on the lines.

1	2	3	4	5	6
7 A	C	D	E	F	G
8 H	I	K	N	O	P
9 R	S	T	U	W	Y

59 18 17 39   37 58   69 58 49   67 47 39   28 57

_____

69 58 49   27 19 58 29 29   17   38 17 48 67 17 19 58 58

_____

17 48 37   17   19 17 27 27 58 58 48 ?   17   57 49 19

_____

27 58 17 39   59 28 39 18   68 58 27 38 47 39 29 .

_____

Answer on page 87.

Eensy-Weensy

Write a letter in the blank space on each line to find a word that means "eensy-weensy." Then read down the starred column to find creatures that are this size.

```
            *
      DI __ INUTIVE
       T __ N Y
  MINUS __ ULE
 MINIATU __ E
  SUBAT __ MIC
   ITTY- __ ITTY
   LITTL __
         __ MALL
```

Answer on page 92.

Bug Off!

19

Find and circle the names of 17 bugs in the grid below. Look across, up, down, and diagonally, both forward and backward. **APHID** has been circled to start you off. After you've found and circled all the words, put the *leftover* letters into the blank spaces below. Keep the letters in order, from left to right and top to bottom, and you'll answer this riddle: What did the mother lightning bug say about her son?

ANT
APHID
BEETLE
CICADA
CRICKET
EARWIG
FRUITFLY
GNAT
HORNET
KATYDID
LADYBUG
LOCUST
MIDGE
TERMITE
TICK
WASP
WEEVIL

```
C H E G U B Y D A L
R I E G I S B P F R
I H C T D G H I R E
C O G A S I N G U L
K R I N D U M A I T
E N W T H A C V T E
T E R M I T E O F E
T T A F I E O R L B
H I E C W A S P Y S
A G K A T Y D I D E
```

Riddle answer:

___ ___ ___ ___ ___ ___ ___ ___ ___ ___ ___ ___ ___ ___ ___

___ ___ ___

Answer on page 94.

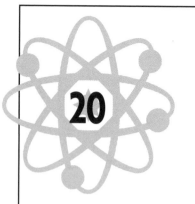

Backing In

20

Figure out the words that answer the clues in the parentheses ( ). Write those words in the blank spaces, but *backwards*, to form on each line the name of a flower.

Example: __ __ __ S Y (short sleep) = P A N S Y (NAP written-in backwards)

1. A M A R Y __ __ __ S (sick)
2. A __ __ __ O N E (grown-up males)
3. __ __ __ E R C U P (bathing place)
4. C A R __ __ __ I O N (make animal skins into leather)
5. C L E M A __ __ __ (use a chair)
6. D A F F O __ __ __ (jar top)
7. __ __ __ D E N I A (cleaning cloth)
8. I M __ __ __ I E N C E (type of dance)
9. I __ __ __ (title for a man)
10. L A V E N __ __ __ (color of tomatoes)
11. __ __ __ I G O L D (male sheep)
12. __ __ __ F L O W E R (sweet potato)
13. __ __ __ C I S S U S (took part in a race)
14. P E R I W I N __ __ __ (big moose)
15. P E __ __ __ I A (cashew, for example)
16. __ __ __ P Y (another name for Dad)
17. S __ __ __ D R A G O N (cooking utensil)
18. S __ __ __ B A L L (came in first in an election)
19. S W __ __ __ __ W I L L I A M (with "off," golfing term)
20. W I S T E __ __ __ (what we breathe)

Answer on page 88.

Name Dropping

Follow the set of instructions below each grid carefully
to find the first and last names of a famous scientist.

B	Y	D	M	C	R	Y	C
Z	M	E	E	R	Z	M	F
A	R	D	D	L	D	F	A
E	A	X	C	G	Y	O	Y
R	U	R	D	A	X	R	Z
C	R	M	B	M	B	Z	C
B	R	B	D	I	R	D	Y
R	M	S	G	B	D	X	B

g	f	f	h	V	K	O	P
Q	A	W	Q	L	i	V	W
K	Q	S	T	K	V	g	b
i	W	L	c	Q	i	J	h
V	E	W	h	Q	x	L	m
Q	K	J	L	W	Q	i	K
h	Q	V	U	L	V	L	W
V	d	J	J	R	W	V	n

1. Cross off the first seven letters
of the alphabet every time
you see them.

2. Cross off the last three letters
of the alphabet every time
you see them.

3. Cross off the 13th letter of the
alphabet every time you see it.

4. Cross off the 18th letter of the
alphabet every time you see it.

5. Write the *unused* letters on
the blank spaces. Keep the
letters in order, from left to
right and top to bottom.

1. Cross off the 10th, 11th, and
12th letters of the alphabet
every time you see them.

2. Cross off all the lower-case
small letters every time you
see them.

3. Cross off every **O**.

4. Cross off every **Q**.

5. Cross off the 22nd and 23rd letters every time you see them.

6. Write the *unused* letters on
the blank spaces. Keep the
letters in order, from left to
right and top to bottom.

__ __ __ __ __ __   __ __ __ __ __ __ __

Answer on page 93.

Scrambled Fact

Unscramble each individual word and write the new words you make on the lines below and you will learn some interesting information.

DRISB LONY PLEES NI STENS HEWN HEYT REA

_____

VANGHI SIBBEA. TA THERO MISTE HYTE SPEEL NAY

_____

CELPA. HYET NAC ZODE NO RETE CHANBERS; YETH

_____

ANC PELSE HELIW NATGINDS TA HET CHABE RO

_____

HEWN HYET REA GLYNIF. HEYT REA BLEA OT OD

_____

SIHT CABSUEE NEO LFAH FO HITER RANIB PESELS

_____

NAD HET THROE LAFH SI AKEWA.

_____

Answer on page 90.

Creature Words

The name of each creature in the right column contains a word that fits the clue in the left-hand column. To find this word, cross off some letters in the creature's name and then read the remaining letters from left to right. Write the new word on the blank space. We did one for you.

Clue	Answer	Creature
1. Opposite of bottom	**TOP**	ANTELOPE
2. Sack		BADGER
3. Ship		BOBCAT
4. Folding bed		COYOTE
5. Tilt		ELEPHANT
6. Material in pencils		LEOPARD
7. Despise		HAMSTER
8. Glass container		JAGUAR
9. Use needle and thread		SHREW
10. Man's neckwear		TIGER
11. A direction		WILDEBEEST
12. Labyrinth		CHIMPANZEE
13. Cook on a barbecue		GORILLA
14. Male child		BISON
15. Contents of socks		FERRET
16. Baby's bed		CARIBOU
17. Bus passenger		REINDEER
18. Opposite of light		AARDVARK

Answer on page 93.

Bright Beginnings

Add a letter in front of each word to make a new word that fits the definition in the parentheses ( ). Then read *down* the column to find the answer to this riddle: What dogs like to help scientists?

___ EARN (get some knowledge)

___ VENUE (street)

___ LACK (color of coal)

___ SCAR (Academy Award statue)

___ EGRET (feel sorry about something)

___ LIKE (similar)

___ HIS (opposite of that)

___ LIVE (type of oil)

___ EMOTE (type of TV control)

___ EARLY (happening once every 365 days)

___ ARE (unusual)

___ BONY (dark wood)

___ HEY (the people)

___ ENTER (person who leases an apartment)

___ DEAL (perfect)

___ VENT (happening)

___ ALLEY (low area between hills)

___ MERGE (come out)

___ EACH (arrive at)

___ KETCH (drawing)

Answer on page 94.

Filling Station #1

An interesting science fact is hidden here. To find it, figure out the answer to each clue below. Then write that word in *two* places—right after the clue and in the puzzle box below (be sure to match up the numbers). Work back and forth between the clues and the "filling station." One word has been entered for you.

Clues

1, 2, 3, 4, 5 = Make a statement **UTTER**

6, 7, 8, 9 = Fibs _____

10, 11, 12 = Strawberry color _____

13, 14, 15, 16 = Monthly payment to a landlord _____

17, 18, 19, 20 = Twelve inches _____

21, 22, 23 = Smack _____

24, 25, 26, 27 = Clean _____

28, 29, 30 = Hearing organ _____

31, 32, 33, 34, 35 = Opposite of wrong _____

36, 37, 38, 39 = The center of an apple _____

40, 41, 42 = Mom's husband _____

43, 44, 45 = Drink that comes in a "bag" _____

46, 47, 48 = Baby bear _____

49, 50, 51 = Used a chair _____

52, 53, 54 = Female chicken _____

55, 56, 57 = Evergreen tree _____

58, 59, 60 = Sides in a dodecahedron _____

B U T T E R F _ _ _ _   A _ _   _ I F F E _ _ _ _
  1 2 3 4 5   6 7 8 9   10 11   12   13 14 15 16

_ R _ M M _ _ _ S _ N _ _ O W _ Y _ .
17 18   19 20 21 22 23 24   25 26

T _ _ Y _ _ E B _ _ _ _ _ L Y _ O L _ _ _ _
27 28 29 30   31 32 33 34 35   36   37 38 39 40

_ N _ _ H _ Y H _ V E _ L _ _ _ _ _ _
41 42 43 44   45 46 47 48 49 50 51

T _ E _ _ D O _ T H E _ _ A N _ _ _ N A E .
52 53 54 55   56 57   58 59 60

Answer on page 87.

1-2-3

26

Find a riddle and its answer in 3 easy steps.

1. Solve each math problem.
2. Refer to the code below and replace the numbered answer with the letter it represents.
3. Read each column from top to bottom. We did one to start you off.

A = 4	B = 5	C = 6	D = 8	E = 9	G = 10
H = 12	I = 15	L = 18	M = 20	N = 21	O = 24
R = 27	S = 30	T = 35	U = 36	W = 40	Y = 45

10 x 4 =   40   =   W

6 x 2 = ___ = ___

9 x 5 = ___ = ___

25 − 10 = ___ = ___

60 − 30 = ___ = ___

18 − 14 = ___ = ___

75 − 40 = ___ = ___

4 x 3 = ___ = ___

3 x 3 = ___ = ___

9 x 3 = ___ = ___

10 x 2 = ___ = ___

8 x 3 = ___ = ___

40 ÷ 2 = ___ = ___

18 ÷ 2 = ___ = ___

70 ÷ 2 = ___ = ___

8 + 1 = ___ = ___

67 − 40 = ___ = ___

95 − 60 = ___ = ___

96 − 84 = ___ = ___

81 ÷ 9 = ___ = ___

4 x 5 = ___ = ___

12 x 2 = ___ = ___

90 ÷ 3 = ___ = ___

90 − 55 = ___ = ___

72 − 63 = ___ = ___

4 x 2 = ___ = ___

9 x 4 = ___ = ___

4 + 2 = ___ = ___

16 ÷ 4 = ___ = ___

85 − 50 = ___ = ___

45 − 36 = ___ = ___

16 − 8 = ___ = ___

33 + 2 = ___ = ___

9 + 3 = ___ = ___

30 ÷ 2 = ___ = ___

7 x 3 = ___ = ___

50 ÷ 5 = ___ = ___

14 + 1 = ___ = ___

30 − 9 = ___ = ___

16 − 12 = ___ = ___

9 x 2 = ___ = ___

24 − 20 = ___ = ___

25 ÷ 5 = ___ = ___ ?

3 x 5 = ___ = ___

37 − 2 = ___ = ___

24 ÷ 2 = ___ = ___

24 ÷ 6 = ___ = ___

60 ÷ 2 = ___ = ___

10 x 3 = ___ = ___

48 ÷ 2 = ___ = ___

80 ÷ 4 = ___ = ___

40 ÷ 10 = ___ = ___

63 ÷ 3 = ___ = ___

90 ÷ 2 = ___ = ___

18 − 10 = ___ = ___

90 − 81 = ___ = ___

90 ÷ 9 = ___ = ___

54 ÷ 2 = ___ = ___

79 − 70 = ___ = ___

72 ÷ 8 = ___ = ___

15 x 2 = ___ = ___

Answer on page 88.

Elementary Fun

Atomic elements are the building blocks of nature. Now you can rebuild the 20 atomic elements listed here. Just take one of the three-letter words from the right-hand column and put it into an empty space in the left-hand column to make the name of an atomic element.

1.	__ __ __ I U M	POT
2.	__ __ __ B O N	TEN
3.	__ __ __ A L T	TAN
4.	__ __ __ P E R	EON
5.	G __ __ __	NIT
6.	I O __ __ __ E	TIN
7.	K R Y P __ __ __	BAR
8.	__ __ __ H I U M	SOD
9.	__ __ __ G A N E S E	COP
10.	M E R __ __ __ Y	FUR
11.	N __ __ __	DIN
12.	__ __ __ R O G E N	MAN
13.	P L A __ __ __ U M	COB
14.	__ __ __ A S S I U M	RAN
15.	__ __ __ I U M	OLD
16.	S U L __ __ __	LIT
17.	T I __ __ __ I U M	CUR
18.	T U N G S __ __ __	TON
19.	U __ __ __ I U M	CON
20.	Z I R __ __ __ I U M	CAR

Answer on page 89.

28 Hot Stuff

Figure out the word that completes each sentence and find it in the same numbered row in the diagram. Cross out the word, letter by letter. All the letters of an answer will always be next to each other, but there will be extra letters on each line. When you're finished, put these *leftover* letters in the spaces below. Work from left to right and top to bottom, and you'll find the name of a hot place in the United States.

1. You should drink a lot of ___ when you're in hot places.
1. A synonym for dry is ___.
2. A caravan stop in a desert is called an ___.
2. A person who travels from place to place in a desert is a ___.
3. A plant that grows in the desert is a ___ . . .
3. . . . and this plant has a long ___ system.
4. Temperatures in the desert could be very hot, or ___.
5. A ___ , a reptile with scaly skin, is found in warm climates.
5. The deserts are filled with ___ . . .
6. . . . and mounds of this material are called ___.
6. Flat-topped hills in warm places like Arizona are called ___.

1	W	A	T	E	R	D	E	A	R	I	D
2	O	A	S	I	S	A	N	O	M	A	D
3	C	A	C	T	U	S	T	R	O	O	T
4	H	S	C	O	R	C	H	I	N	G	V
5	L	I	Z	A	R	D	A	S	A	N	D
6	L	D	U	N	E	S	M	E	S	A	S
7	F	L	A	S	H	F	L	O	O	D	L
8	W	I	N	D	S	T	O	R	M	S	E
9	C	A	M	E	L	S	Y	G	O	B	I

7. A short and intense rainfall can lead to a ___ ___.
8. Other dangers in the desert are ___.
9. People travel through the desert on ___.
9. The ___ Desert is in Mongolia and China.

Answer: ___ ___ ___ ___ ___   ___ ___ ___ ___ ___ ___

Answer on page 90.

Criss-Crossing Mammals

A mammal is a warm-blooded animal with a backbone. It usually has fur or hair on its body. Put each mammal on the list into the grid. One mammal is already in place to get you started.

3 Letters
COW
FOX
PIG
RAT
YAK

4 Letters
GOAT
HARE
MULE
VOLE

5 Letters
CAMEL
KOALA
LLAMA
MOOSE
PANDA
TIGER

6 Letters
ALPACA
BADGER
BEAVER
ERMINE
RABBIT

7 Letters
CHEETAH
GIRAFFE
MUSKRAT
PANTHER
RACCOON

8 Letters
ANTELOPE
HEDGEHOG

Answer on page 92.

30 Scientist's Snack

Write a letter in the blank space on each line to complete the name of a snack food. Then read *downward* under the starred column to find the answer to this riddle: What is an atomic scientist's favorite snack?

```
                    *
              __  U D G E
      C O O K __  E
        P A __  T R Y
              __  H E R B E T
      B R O W N __  E
            P __  P C O R N
        C A __  D Y


              __  A K E
    D O U G __  N U T
          L __  C O R I C E
              __  R E T Z E L
        B I __  C U I T
```

Answer on page 93.

General Science

Some terms used by scientists are in the list below. To find them, figure out the answer to the clue in the parentheses ( ) on the left. Then write that word in the empty spaces on each line to find the word that answers the clue in the brackets [ ] on the right.

1. (cult) I N __ __ __ __ I C I D E [poisonous spray used on plants]
2. (ripped) __ __ __ __ A D O [twister]
3. (get into picture position) D E C O M __ __ __ __ [break down into small pieces]
4. (bee's home) S __ __ __ __ R I N G [the body's reaction to cold]
5. (what you wear over pajamas) M I C __ __ __ __ S [tiny living creatures]
6. (handle a difficult situation) M I C R O S __ __ __ __ [instrument with a lens]
7. (object that rings) C E R E __ __ __ __ U M [part of the brain]
8. (a fixed price) E V A P O __ __ __ __ [change from a liquid to a gas]
9. (cooking vessel) H Y __ __ __ H E S I S [a careful guess]
10. (edge) E X P E __ __ __ E N T [a scientific test]
11. (play a part) B __ __ __ E R I A [germs]
12. (take the bus) S O D I U M C H L O __ __ __ __ [salt]
13. (walking stick) H U R R I __ __ __ __ [powerful storm]
14. (let fall) H Y __ __ __ __ O N I C S [science of farming without soil]
15. (in this place) A T M O S P __ __ __ __ [the air surrounding the earth]
16. (pocket bread) P R E C I __ __ __ __ T I O N [rain, snow, sleet, etc.]
17. (burrowing animal) __ __ __ __ C U L E S [tiny bits of matter]
18. (endure) S A N D B __ __ __ __ I N G [method of cleaning stone buildings]
19. (shopping area) S __ __ __ __ P O X [serious contagious disease]
20. (almond or pecan) __ __ __ R I E N T S [food elements needed for growth]

Answer on page 87.

32 Food Experiments

Become a mad scientist in the kitchen and experiment with your food to make new items. Just add or subtract the letters given on each line to/from the food listed, then rearrange those letters to form new words that fit the clues in the parentheses ( ).

Example: CEREAL − E = (evident) = CLEAR

1. YAM + RR = (wed) = _____
2. FISH + T = (switch gears) = _____
3. VEAL + E = (go away) = _____
4. BAGEL + SE = (dogs like Snoopy) = _____
5. EGGPLANT − GG = (Pluto or Mercury) = _____
6. BROWNIE − WE = (red bird) = _____
7. OYSTERS − YT = (red flowers) = _____
8. PARSLEY − Y = (necklace beads) = _____
9. SCALLION − NO = (purple flowers) = _____
10. ORANGE − E = (react to a corny riddle) = _____
11. NECTARINE − ER = (very old) = _____
12. TURNIP − U = (write in block letters) = _____
13. PEANUTS − AN = (disturbed) = _____
14. LIME + S = (grin) = _____
15. OKRA + C = (frog sound) = _____
16. KALE + SR = (Los Angeles basketball team) = _____
17. ONION − I = (12 o'clock) = _____
18. NECTAR − N = (respond) = _____
19. CASHEW − A = (chomps on gum) _____
20. CHOWDER − HE = (large group of people) = _____

Answer on page 88.

Problem Solving

Follow the directions on each line very carefully and you'll change a problem for some animals (like bears) into a solution.

1. Write LACKOFFOOD without word spacing _____
2. Change "A" to letter following it in the alphabet _____
3. Change "OFF" to "AT" _____
4. Change the second vowel to "I" _____
5. Change the third consonant to "R" _____
6. Change the fourth consonant to "N" _____
7. Get rid of the first letter _____
8. Change the last letter to "N" _____
9. Place an "E" between the first two consonants _____
10. Place "HI" before the first letter _____

Answer on page 89.

Read It!

Write a letter in the blank space on each line to spell out something that can be read. Then read *down* the starred column to find another type of reading material.

```
          *
      __  A G A
   S  __  R I P T
 T H R __  L L E R
      __  P I C
 R O M A __  C E
 A N E __  D O T E
   R __  P O R T


      __  A B L E
 M E M O __  R
 C O M I __  S
      __  A L E
   D __  A R Y
   N __  V E L
 Y A R __
```

Answer on page 91.

Job Search

Join together two 3-letter pieces from the box to make a 6-letter word that answers each clue. Write the word into the grid, reading *downward*. After you use each 3-letter piece, cross it off. Then, when the grid is complete, read *across* the starred rows to find a scientist's co-worker.

ANS	BAS	CAT	COL	ECT
ING	LIE	MAN	MON	NIP
NTS	OBJ	ORG	PLA	RCH
SET	STA	THS	TRU	TYP

	1	2	3	4	5	6	7	8	9	10
★										
★										

1. Botanists study these living things
2. A kind of hound with drooping ears
3. A real thing
4. What May and June are
5. What hearts and livers are
6. Treat for a kitten
7. Potatoes and rice contain this food substance
8. A dog like Lassie
9. President Harry S. ___
10. Using a keyboard on a computer

Answer on page 93.

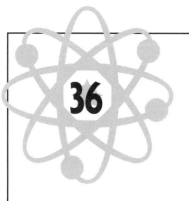

36 Opposite Distraction

Fill in the blank spaces with a word that means *the opposite of* the word inside the brackets [ ] at the left. The new word you make will name a scientist whose accomplishment is described inside the parentheses ( ) at the right.

1. [weak]   A R M __ __ __ __ __ __ (first person to walk on the moon)
2. [lose]   D A R __ __ __ (developed theory of evolution)
3. [live]   __ __ __ S E L (built engine that bears his name)
4. [near]   __ __ __ A D A Y (made the first generator)
5. [nothing] H __ __ __ E Y (identified a comet that bears his name)
6. [his]   __ __ __ __ __ C H E L (discovered the planet Uranus)
7. [high]   __ __ __ __ E L L (predicted the position of the ninth planet, Pluto)
8. [sick]   M A X __ __ __ __ (worked on magnetism)
9. [begin]   M __ __ __ E L (did experiments on heredity)
10. [old]   __ __ __ T O N (discovered laws of gravity)
11. [present] __ __ __ __ __ E U R (developed milk sterilization process)
12. [against] R U T H E R __ __ __ D (discovered the atomic nucleus)
13. [peace]   D E __ __ __ (first to liquify hydrogen)
14. [left]   W __ __ __ __ __ BROTHERS (flew the first airplane)

Answer on page 92.

Lost Letters

One letter was "lost" from each word in the list before it was put in the grid. Example: **STABLE** is in the list, but the **B** was lost and **STALE** was circled in the grid. To find the lost letters and each new word, look across, up, down, forward, backward, and diagonally. Write the lost letter on the line and circle the new word in the grid. (Note: Don't let a few alternate-answer words trip you up. You won't find them in the grid.) When you've found all the words, read the lost letters from **1** to **29** to answer this riddle: Why are bacteria bad at math?

1. STABLE **B**
2. BEACON ___
3. FACULTY ___
4. BOARDER ___
5. DURESS ___
6. THIRSTY ___
7. FEATHER ___
8. STURGEON ___
9. PHEASANT ___
10. FEASTS ___
11. TRYOUT ___
12. CLAMPS ___
13. SPOUT ___
14. COMPLETE ___
15. MORTAL ___
16. MAIZE ___
17. INSPECT ___
18. FLIGHT ___
19. FLYING ___
20. TIMBER ___
21. READYING ___

22. POWDER ___
23. COPIES ___
24. SOLVE ___
25. WIRING ___

26. MINDED ___
27. PHONIES ___
28. MENTAL ___
29. BRIDGE ___

```
S P E A S A N T S T R S T
U R E W O P L C N G C T H
R B R K L D R E S S O S G
G P E B E L S S P H M A I
E N M N Z S E N O H P F F
O G I Q B T Z I T X E A L
N M T R E A D I N G T U I
M A Z E W L C M M H E L N
B R I D E E O O E V Q T G
T H I R T Y P R N T Z Y R
L T U O R T E V C L A P S
N M Y B W X S M O R A L Z
```

Answer on page 95.

Material Things

Unscramble each word and put it into the grid. Then read down the starred column to see what you should do with this stuff.

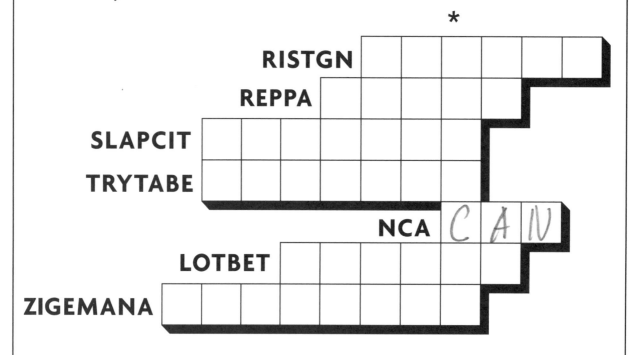

RISTGN

REPPA

SLAPCIT

TRYTABE

NCA C A N

LOTBET

ZIGEMANA

Answer on page 87.

Circulation Fact

Answer each clue and write the answers on the numbered spaces. Then move the numbered letters to the same-numbered spaces in the answer section below. Work back and forth between the clues and the answer section to find an important fact about circulation.

Clues

A. Type of school for three-year-olds

__ __ __ __ __ __ __
19 22 7 47 56 61 51

B. Tossed veggie dish __ __ __ __ __
54 44 64 40 20

C. Belonging to me __ __ __ __
57 25 9 16

D. Twelve o'clock __ __ __ __
27 31 4 41

E. Move like a worm __ __ __ __ __ __
52 62 10 15 2 26

F. Chore __ __ __ __
30 63 39 45

G. Cures __ __ __ __ __
33 46 50 37 11

H. Precise __ __ __ __ __
60 13 48 35 28

I. Not tight __ __ __ __ __
38 12 3 65 34

J. Ties up (rhymes with "minds")

__ __ __ __ __
1 8 17 42 29

K. Cuckoo (rhymes with "catty")

__ __ __ __ __
6 18 23 59 14

L. Be present at an event

__ __ __ __ __ __
58 55 43 36 21 5

M. Small lump on the skin

__ __ __ __
49 53 24 32

Answer:

__ __ __ __ __ __ __ __ __ __ __ __ __ __ __ __ __
1 2 3 4 5   6 7 8 9 10 11   12 13 14 15 16 17

__ __ __ __ __ __ __ __ __ __ __ __ __ __ __
18 19 20 21 22 23 24 25 26 27 28 29 30 31 32 33 34

__ __ __ __ __ __ __ __ __ __ __ __ __ __ __ __ __
35 36 37 38 39 40 41 42 43 44 45 46 47 48 49 50 51

__ __ __ __ __ __ __ __ __ __ __ __ __ __.
52 53 54 55 56 57 58 59 60 61 62 63 64 65

Answer on page 89

Criss-Crossing Body Parts

Place each body part into the diagram in the one spot where it belongs. Cross off each word after you place it, because it will only be used once. We put in a few letters to get you going. Watch out! There are some tricky spots!

3 Letters
ARM
EAR
EYE
LEG
LIP

4 Letters
BONE
HAND
HEAD
KNEE
NAIL
NOSE

5 Letters
AORTA
BRAIN
ELBOW
HEART
LIVER
SPINE
WAIST

6 Letters
FINGER
SPLEEN
THORAX
TONGUE

7 Letters
STOMACH
TONSILS
TRACHEA

8 Letters
ADENOIDS
APPENDIX
PANCREAS
SHOULDER

Answer on page 90.

Scientific Research #1

The name of each scientist in the right column contains a word that fits the clue in the left column. To find this word, cross off some letters in the scientist's name and then read the remaining letters from left to right.

	Example: Money	CASH	CAVENDISH

Clue	Answer	Scientist
1. Type of bed	_____	BURBANK
2. Fishing rod	_____	PTOLEMY
3. Bear's home	_____	CARVER
4. Crusted dessert	_____	OPPENHEIMER
5. Female deer	_____	DOOLEY
6. Cooling device	_____	FEYNMAN
7. Strong wind	_____	GALILEO
8. Type of phone	_____	MITCHELL
9. Heal	_____	CURIE
10. Relax	_____	PRIESTLEY
11. Spoil	_____	ROENTGEN
12. Baby farm animal	_____	CHADWICK
13. Matador's cape color	_____	REED
14. Young boy	_____	LAND
15. Lock opener	_____	KENNY
16. Map	_____	CHARCOT
17. School vehicle	_____	BUNSEN

Answer on page 94.

Found Letters #1

What did the mad scientist get when he made an exact duplicate of Texas? For the answer to this riddle, find the one letter in the word in the right-hand column that's *not* in the word in the left-hand column. Write the extra letter on the blank space. Then read *down* the column.

RIVER	___	ARRIVE
MAILED	___	DECIMAL
AGENT	___	TANGLE
BLEND	___	BLONDE
GRATES	___	STRANGE
SNAIL	___	ALIENS
DRAPES	___	SPREADS
PERIL	___	TRIPLE
HOTEL	___	LOATHE
SHAPE	___	PHRASE
TRAIT	___	ARTIST
MARES	___	STREAM
TALLER	___	LATERAL
VEINS	___	INVEST
TRACE	___	CREATE

Answer on page 87.

Inside Outer Space

Each sentence below contains a word that is associated with the science of astronomy, but it is hidden. Underline each word, when you find it. Ignore spacing and punctuation.

Example: IS THE BRON<u>COS' MOS</u>COW TRIP CANCELLED?

1. THERE ARE SEVEN USED CARS IN THE DRIVEWAY.
2. WHO WANTS A TURNOVER FOR DESSERT?
3. DID YOU HEAR THAT JOKE ABOUT THE CLOWN?
4. PLEASE COME TO MY PARTY.
5. WE'LL VISIT THE ALAMO ON FRIDAY.
6. TIME TO WORK ON YOUR GRAMMAR, SON.
7. HE'S AN INEPT, UNEDUCATED RAT!
8. THE STATION IS JUST AROUND THE CORNER.
9. AL PACINO VACATIONED THERE.
10. THIS UNUSUAL PAINTING IS ON SALE.
11. THE PLANE TAXIED DOWN THE RUNWAY.

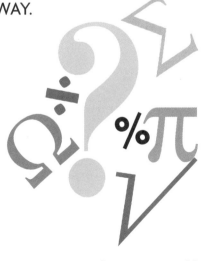

Answer on page 88.

Same Starts #1

Each group of scientific words starts with the same three letters (which may or may not be a real word). Use the clues in the parentheses ( ) to help you decide which letters to place in the blanks.

1. __ __ __ O M (snake's poison)
   __ __ __ U S (second planet from the sun)
   __ __ __ I S O N (deer meat)

2. __ __ __ A S S I U M (silver-white metal used
      in making fertilizer)
   __ __ __ A T O (vegetable that grows underground)
   __ __ __ E N T (strong, like a vaccine)

3. __ __ __ A B O L I S M (activities that living things
      do to stay alive)
   __ __ __ R I C (type of measurement system)
   __ __ __ H O D (scientific procedure)

4. __ __ __ C E R (harmful disease)
   __ __ __ N I B A L (person who eats human flesh)
   __ __ __ Y O N (deep valley with high sides)

5. __ __ __ L B L A D D E R (body organ near the liver)
   __ __ __ L O N (liquid measurement)
   __ __ __ A P A G O S (islands where many endangered
      species live)

6. __ __ __ C I U M (essential ingredient for teeth)
   __ __ __ O R I E S (measuring units for the amount of
      heat in something)
   __ __ __ L U S (hard spot on the skin)

7. __ __ __ O N (wading bird)
__ __ __ R I N G (small fish)
__ __ __ E D I T Y (process of passing traits from parent to child)

8. __ __ __ R E S T (world's highest mountain)
__ __ __ R G L A D E S (swampy area in Florida)
__ __ __ R G R E E N (type of tree)

9. __ __ __ R I F I E D (like wood that has turned to stone)
__ __ __ R O L E U M (material used for making fuel)
__ __ __ R I   D I S H (item used for the study of bacteria)

10. __ __ __ A L T (metallic element used in alloys)
__ __ __ W E B (spider's product)
__ __ __ R A (poisonous snake)

11. __ __ __ M P A N Z E E (ape)
__ __ __ P M U N K (small animal related to the squirrel)
__ __ __ C K E N P O X (common childhood disease)

12. __ __ __ R F I S H (sea animal with five arms)
__ __ __ R C H (what rice and potatoes contain)
__ __ __ M I N A (endurance)

Answer on page 89.

45 Throw It Out!

Use the grid below and cross out a word or phrase that names a food or part of a food that you would throw out. Example: On the first line you would cross out **ORANGE RIND**. There will always be some extra letters left on each line after you cross out these words. When you're done, read these *remaining* letters from left to right and top to bottom. You will discover the first stage of what goes on at a garbage dump. To find out the rest of what happens, just read the sentence below the grid from left to right. All the words are in the correct order; you just have to figure out the correct spacing.

M	I	O	R	A	N	G	E	R	I	N	D
C	H	I	C	K	E	N	B	O	N	E	C
R	O	B	A	N	A	N	A	P	E	E	L
A	P	P	L	E	C	O	R	E	B	E	S
C	P	E	A	C	H	P	I	T	R	U	M
B	L	S	T	A	L	E	B	R	E	A	D
M	O	L	D	Y	C	H	E	E	S	E	E
F	O	O	E	G	G	S	H	E	L	L	D
F	I	S	H	B	O	N	E	I	N	T	O
P	O	T	A	T	O	S	K	I	N	T	I
N	Y	C	L	A	M	S	H	E	L	L	B
G	R	A	P	E	S	E	E	D	I	T	S

THE SEBI TSTH ENTUR NINT OGAS, APR OCES SCAL

LEDD ECO MPO SITI ON, ORSIM PLYR OT TING.

Answer on page 90.

48

5s, 6s, 7s, 8s

Insert a letter in the blank space on each line to make a common 5-letter word. Then read down the center column to find the name of a science.

TO __ A Z
US __ E R
KA __ A K
O N __ E T
S K __ M P
P R __ V E
H E __ L O
C L __ W N
O U __ H T
M A __ B E

QUA __ T E R
CAB __ O S E
RES __ E C T
ARC __ E R Y
ACR __ L I C
BLO __ S O M
DEL __ G H T
CRA __ K L E
MES __ A G E

... again, with 6-letter words

PLA __ M A
SCR __ L L
CAT __ H Y
SQU __ N T
ROB __ T S
VAL __ E Y
CHR __ M E
BEG __ A R
CRA __ O N

... last, with 8-letter words

ADO __ T I O N
AQU __ R I U M
WET __ A N D S
SCH __ D U L E
PAN __ R A M A
TRA __ S M I T
FAI __ H F U L
PAL __ M I N O
DWE __ L I N G
THE __ R I E S
GAR __ O Y L E
PLA __ T I M E

... now, with 7-letter words

EXH __ U S T
PAR __ L E Y
INS __ E A D

Answer on page 91

Ear-ing Aid

Humans and animals use their ears for hearing. There's an EAR on each line below and it's part of a longer word. Fill in the blanks with letters to form words that answer the clues, and you'll be able to EAR perfectly!

1. __ __ __ E A R __ __ __ __ = the way a person or thing looks
2. __ E A R __ = hair growth on a man's face
3. __ __ E A R __ __ __ = space in a forest without any trees or bushes
4. E A R __ __ = opposite of late
5. E A R __ __ __ __ = serious and sincere
6. E A R __ __ __ __ __ = jewelry worn on the lobes
7. E A R __ __ __ __ __ __ __ = strong shaking of the ground
8. E A R __ __ __ __ __ __ = small, wriggly creature that lives in the soil
9. __ E A R __ __ __ = closest
10. __ E A R __ __ = round gems found in oysters
11. __ __ __ E A R __ __ __ = practice performance of a play
12. __ __ __ E A R __ __ __ __ = person who studies or tests things
13. __ __ E A R = remove wool from a sheep
14. __ __ E A R = weapon used to catch fish
15. __ __ E A R = make a serious promise
16. __ E A R __ __ __ = ripping

Answer on page 87.

Filling Station #2 48

An interesting science fact is hidden here. To find it, figure out the answer to each clue. Then write that word in *two* places—after the clue and again in the numbered blanks below, being sure to match-up the numbers. Work back and forth between the clues and the "filling station." One word has been entered for you.

Clues

1, 2, 3, 4 = Vegetable on the cob **CORN**

5, 6, 7, 8 = Fiber used to make rope _____

9, 10, 11, 12 = A fixed price _____

13, 14, 15, 16 = Every _____

17, 18, 19 = Woman who lives in a convent _____

20, 21, 22 = Color of beets _____

23, 24, 25, 26 = Soil _____

27, 28, 29 = Mist _____

30, 31, 32 = Male child _____

33, 34, 35 = Allow _____

36, 37 = Opposite of out _____

38, 39, 40 = Letter after ess _____

41, 42, 43, 44 = End of the arm _____

45, 46, 47 = Definite article _____

IN C A L I F O R N I A   T _ _ _   T E _ _ E _ _ _ U R _
       1   2 3 4   5 6   7 8 9 10 11 12

R _ _ _ _ _ E D   O _ E   H _ _ D _ _ _ _   A N _   T H _ _ _ Y–
13 14 15 16   17   18 19 20 21 22   23   24 25 26

_ _ U R   D E _ R E E _   _ _ _   J U _ Y   T _ N _ H
27 28   29   30 31 32   33   34 35

N _ _ E _ _ _ _ N   _ U N D R E D   _ _ _ _   _ _ I R T _ E N.
36 37 38 39 40   41   42 43 44 45 46   47

Answer on page 89.

Seeing Stars

The names of 10 constellations are scattered around this page. Put them into the grid in alphabetical order and then read down the starred column. You'll find the type of scientist who studies stars and other heavenly bodies.

49

PISCES

SCORPIO

INDUS

*

DRACO

DORADO

ARGO

ARIES

MUSCA

CETUS

LEO

Answer on page 88

Some Fisherman!

Fill in the blank space on each line to spell the name of a fish. Then read down the starred column to find the name of a scientist who studies fish.

50

```
                        *
               P __  K E
               __  A R P
           S   __  A R K
           S   __  U R G E O N
           W   __  I T I N G
     A N C H O V __
       H A D D __  C K
           S A __  M O N
           T R __  U T
         P O R __  Y
         H A L __  B U T
         B A S __
               __  U N A
```

Answer on page 90.

Creature Body Parts #1

Here's an amazing scientific discovery. You can add the same two letters to partial words to create a creature and a body part. Just take a 2-letter piece from the box below and place it in the blank spaces on each line to make the *ending* of a creature's name and the *beginning* of a body part. We did the first one for you. Cross off each 2-letter piece as you use it.

AB	AD	AN	AR	CH
EY	FE	LE	NA	NE
SP	S̶T̶	TE	TH	TO

1. L O C U / **S T** / O M A C H
2. J A G U / __ __ / M S
3. G I R A F / __ __ / E T
4. C R / __ __ / D O M E N
5. T U R K / __ __ / E B R O W
6. W H A / __ __ / G S
7. S W / __ __ / K L E
8. S A R D I / __ __ / C K
9. F I N / __ __ / I N
10. W A / __ __ / I N E
11. I G U A / __ __ / V E L
12. M O / __ __ / I G H
13. M O S Q U I / __ __ / E S
14. T E R M I / __ __ / E T H
15. T O / __ __ / E N O I D S

Answer on page 93.

Mini Fill-Ins #2

Complete each grid by putting the words into the spaces where they belong.

Herbs

BASIL
DILL
FENNEL
PARSLEY
ROSEMARY
SAGE
TARRAGON
THYME

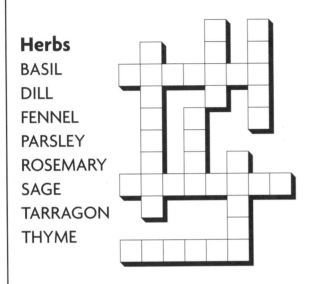

Jeweler's Materials

BERYL
DIAMOND
GOLD
JADE
RUBY
SILVER

Weather Words

BREEZE   SLEET
MIST   SNOW
RAIN   SUN

Tree Parts

BARK   LEAF
BLOSSOM   LIMB
BRANCH   ROOT
FLOWER   TRUNK

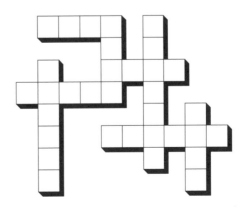

Answer on page 88.

Letter Switch

53

To find a riddle, change each letter below to the one that comes *1 space before it* in the alphabet. Write the words on the lines.

X I B U   J T   U I F   C F T U   X B Z   U P

_____

D B U D I   B   T R V J S S F M?

_____

To find the answer to this riddle, change each letter to the one that comes *2 spaces before it* in the alphabet. Write the words on the lines.

E N K O D   W R   C   V T G G   C P F

_____

C E V   N K M G   C   P W V.

_____

Answer on page 87

Close Relatives #2

54

Change one letter in each word to find four words that belong together in each group. Write the new words on the lines. The first one is done for you.

1. Face Parts
SAW **JAW**
SOUTH _____
CREEK _____
SIPS _____

2. Flowers
DAIRY _____
NOSE _____
SWEEP TEA _____
LILT ON THY GALLEY _____

3. Trees
SEEPING PILLOW _____
LATE BALM _____
SHERRY _____
MINE _____

4. Fruits
DRAPE _____
SLUM _____
TEACH _____
AMPLE _____

5. Deer
DAWN _____
SLAG _____
GOOSE _____
ILK _____

6. Horses
POSY _____
SCALLION _____
BOLT _____
MARK _____

7. Leg Parts
ANGLE _____
KNEW _____
FORT _____
THIN _____

8. Arm Parts
WHIST _____
HANK _____
LINGER _____
BUNNY ZONE _____

9. Meats
PARK _____
STEAM _____
DEAL _____
LAME _____

10. Vegetables
SEAS _____
LAMA JEANS _____
STRONG DEANS _____
SQUISH _____

11. Seasons
SIMMER _____
TINTER _____
FULL _____
STRING _____

12. Body Organs
RIVER _____
RUNGS _____
HEARD _____
DRAIN _____

Answer on page 88.

55 Create-a-Creature

You can be a really mad scientist and create a creature. Here's the formula: On each line, use the word and letter given and scramble the letters to make the creature described. All letters will be used. Write the creature's name on the blank spaces.

Example: TAG + O = Farm animal with short horns = <u>GOAT</u>

1. STREAM + H = Small, furry rodent = _____
2. ORDEAL + P = Wild animal with spots = _____
3. KIN + M = Animal valued for its fur = _____
4. RIPE + V = Poisonous snake = _____
5. BRAVE + E = Animal that builds dams = _____
6. MINER + E = Animal valued for its fur = _____
7. HERS + W = Very small animal similar to a mouse = _____
8. UTTER + L = Reptile that travels with its own house = _____
9. LAME + C = Desert animal with a hump = _____
10. WINS + E = Pigs or hogs = _____
11. RASH + K = Saltwater fish that's dangerous to humans = _____
12. LEASE + W = Small animal with thick fur = _____
13. ROB + A = Wild hog = _____
14. TIRE + G = Striped wild animal = _____
15. DOT + A = Animal related to the frog = _____
16. OPPOSER + I = Sea animal that looks like a small whale = _____
17. GLEE + A = Bird of prey = _____
18. PENCIL + A = Large bird with a long bill = _____
19. NEAR + V = Large black bird = _____
20. ROBE + X = Type of dog = _____
21. PLANES + I = Type of dog = _____
22. TICKER + C = Insect with long legs = _____
23. HOT + M = Insect similar to a butterfly = _____
24. RAZE + B = Black-and-white-striped animal = _____

Answer on page 90.

Criss-Crossing Fish

Place the name of each fish into the one spot where it will fit in the grid. Cross off each fish after you position it. One word has been filled in to get you going.

3 Letters
COD
EEL
RAY

4 Letters
HAKE
LING
SOLE
TUNA

5 Letters
GUPPY
LOACH
SHARK
SKATE
SPRAT
WAHOO

6 Letters
MARLIN
MINNOW
REDFIN

7 Letters
ANCHOVY
LAMPREY
PIRANHA
POMPANO
WALLEYE

8 Letters
ALBACORE
PICKEREL

9 Letters
BARRACUDA
STEELHEAD

S P R A T

Answer on page 89.

Stormy Scientists

Find and circle 18 synonyms for "angry" in the grid below. Look across, up, down, and diagonally, both forward and backward. **ANGRY** has been circled to start you off. After you've found and circled all the words, put the *leftover* letters into the blank spaces below. Keep the letters in order, from left to right and top to bottom, and you'll answer this riddle: What do astronauts do when they get angry?

ANGRY
BITTER
BUGGED
CROSS
DISGUSTED
FIERCE
FIERY
FURIOUS
INCENSED
IRRITATED
LIVID
MAD
RAGING
RILED
SORE
TROUBLED
UPSET
VEXED

```
D  R  I  L  E  D  I  V  I  L
E  I  D  E  L  B  U  O  R  T
S  T  S  G  N  I  G  A  R  F
N  B  H  G  F  B  E  Y  I  I
E  I  A  B  U  P  S  E  T  E
C  T  N  G  R  S  R  L  A  R
N  T  G  S  I  Y  T  A  T  C
I  E  R  S  O  T  O  E  E  E
D  R  Y  F  U  R  M  A  D  F
C  R  O  S  S  D  E  X  E  V
```

Riddle answer: _ _ _ _ _   _ _ _ _ _   _ _ _

Answer on page 93.

Center Line

Put one letter into each blank space to spell a common 7-letter word. Then, read down the starred column to answer this riddle: What kind of jokes did Einstein make?

Now do the same thing with these words to answer another riddle: What snack food do geologists like?

*

ANS __ ERS

SHR __ VEL

BLI __ TER

PAL __ TTE

KNU __ KLE

IMP __ OVE

FAN __ TIC

TEA __ HER

MAN __ IND

PEA __ ANT

*

EME __ ALD

DEP __ SIT

WEL __ OME

BOO __ LET

HAT __ HET

ADV __ NCE

GRA __ ITE

SAN __ BAR

COP __ CAT

Answer on page 90.

Same Starts #2

Each group of scientific words starts with the same three letters (which may or may not be a real word). Use the clues in the parentheses ( ) to help you decide which letters to place in the blanks.

1. _ _ _ T O P L A S M (basic substance of cells)
   _ _ _ T O N (particle of an atom)
   _ _ _ T O Z O A (tiny one-celled animals)
   _ _ _ T E I N (substance found in eggs and meat)

2. _ _ _ A (state of unconsciousness)
   _ _ _ P A S S (instrument that shows directions)
   _ _ _ P U T E R (electronic machine)
   _ _ _ P O U N D (substance formed by two or more elements)

3. _ _ _ K (scientist who developed the polio vaccine)
   _ _ _ A M A N D E R (amphibian)
   _ _ _ M O N (type of fish)
   _ _ _ I V A (mouth fluid that helps in digesting food)

4. _ _ _ C E C R A F T (vehicle used by astronauts)
   _ _ _ S M (sudden uncontrolled movement)
   _ _ _ N I E L (type of dog)
   _ _ _ R R O W (type of bird)

5. _ _ _ B O N (chemical element found in all living things)
   _ _ _ D I O L O G I S T (heart specialist)
   _ _ _ I B O U (a large deer)
   _ _ _ R I E R (a type of pigeon, today extinct)

6. _ _ _ _ D A R I N (type of orange)
_ _ _ _ G O (juicy tropical fruit)
_ _ _ _ G A N E S E (metal used in making steel)
_ _ _ _ A T E E (tropical sea creature)

7. _ _ _ _ D E R (web maker)
_ _ _ _ N A C H (Popeye's favorite veggie)
_ _ _ _ N E (backbone)
_ _ _ _ T Z (type of dog)

8. _ _ _ _ E T A H (fastest-moving land animal)
_ _ _ _ M I S T R Y (science that studies different substances)
_ _ _ _ C K U P (medical examination)
_ _ _ _ M O T H E R A P Y (type of treatment for serious diseases)

9. _ _ _ _ C I E S (a category of related organisms)
_ _ _ _ C T R U M (the bands of color in a rainbow)
_ _ _ _ A R M I N T (flavoring used in chewing gum)
_ _ _ _ L U N K E R (person who explores caves)

10. _ _ _ _ K A (hooded jacket worn at the South Pole)
_ _ _ _ S L E Y (small green plant used as a flavoring)
_ _ _ _ S N I P (veggie that has a thick root)
_ _ _ _ T R I D G E (bird with a fat body)

11. _ _ _ _ N A C L E (small shellfish that attaches itself to rocks)
_ _ _ _ O M E T E R (weather instrument)
_ _ _ _ L E Y (healthy grain)
_ _ _ _ K (tree covering)

12. _ _ _ _ E C A S T (weather prediction)
_ _ _ _ E S T (wooded area)
_ _ _ _ M U L A (healthy drink for babies)
_ _ _ _ T I F Y (add a substance to food to make it more nutritious)

Answer on page 93.

Simile Scramble

A simile is a phrase that compares one thing to another using the words "like" or "as." The simile "strong as an ox" suggests that someone has the strength of an ox. Each simile here contains the name of a creature. Unscramble the two capitalized words in each line below to form a common simile. Write the unscrambled words on the lines.

1. PHYAP as a RALK _____
2. DMA as a HETRON _____
3. LIBDN as a TAB _____
4. UGHRYN as a ABRE _____
5. LYS as a OFX _____
6. ERD as a BOLREST _____
7. SOLEO as a SOGOE _____
8. GRAEE as a REVABE _____
9. LOWS as a LISAN _____
10. LEGNET as a MALB _____
11. LOBD as a NOLI _____
12. ZARCY as a ONOL _____
13. ISEW as an OLW _____
14. UPROD as a COPEKAC _____
15. ETIQU as a SUMOE _____
16. TAF as a GPI _____
17. ABDL as an ALEEG _____
18. BUNTROBS as a LUME _____
19. AWKE as a TINKET _____
20. SYBU as a EEB _____

Answer on page 92.

Squish Squash

There are two related words on each line. All the letters are in the correct order, but the words are squished together. You have to separate them to find the two terms. There's a clue given with each set of words, for example:

Medical students: I R E N S I D T E R N E N T = INTERN and **RESIDENT**

1. Vegetables: L C A E T B B T U A G E C E = _____

2. Stomach: B A B E L D O L Y M E N = _____

3. Gases: H E R A L I D U M O N = _____

4. Endangered species: C O W O N D L O R S V E S = _____

5. Diseases: M E M U A S L M E S P S = _____

6. Senses: T A T S O T U E C H = _____

7. Metals: Z N I C I N K E L C = _____

8. Cats: S I P A E R M S I A E S E N = _____

9. Grazing land: M P A S E A D T U O R E W = _____

10. Apes: G G O I R I B L B L O N A = _____

11. Planets: M J U E P I R C T U R Y E R = _____

12. Water parts: H Y O X Y D R G E N O G E N = _____

13. Oceans: P A I N C I F D I A I C N = _____

14. Snakes: C O P Y N S T R T H I C T O R O N _____

15. Eye parts: L P E U N P S I L _____

16. Carbohydrates: S T S U A R C G A R H _____

17. Fruits: T A C A N T N G E A L R I O U N E P E _____

18. Nuts: P I S F I T A L B C H I O E R T _____

Answer on page 89.

Museum Guide

Here's a write-it-yourself travel guide for an outdoor museum. Some of the words have blank spaces in them, followed by a number in parentheses ( ). To fill in the blanks with the correct words, do the following: First, read the clue on the page opposite that matches the number given. Second, figure out the answer word. Third, write this word in the same-numbered space.

Example: Clue number **1** on the right-hand page says "Opposite of against." The answer, FOR, when placed in the blank spaces for **(1)** below, spells out CaliFORnia.

In Northern Cali __ __ __ nia **(1)** there is a special attraction, Monterey Bay National __ __ rine **(2)** Sanctuary, which gets millions of vi __ __ __ ors **(3)** a year. These tourists watch the otters, harbor seals and birds that splash on the b __ __ __ __ es **(4)**. T__ __ __ __ y-six **(5)** species of aquatic mammals live in the sanctuary, including bottle __ __ __ __ **(6)** dolphins. There are also many types of inverte __ __ __ __ es **(7)**.

A popular feature is the undersea __ __ __ yon **(8)**. Some of the things you can see are the sea otters who dive under the surface to find creatures like abal __ __ __ **(9)** and sea ur __ __ __ __ s **(10)**. Otters are closely related to w __ __ __ __ __ __ **(11)**. They were al__ __ __ __ **(12)** wiped out in the early 1900s by fur t __ __ __ pers **(13)**, but they were put on the U.S. En __ __ __ __ __ __ ed **(14)** Species List and are now making a comeback. You can also watch the seals zip a __ __ __ __ **(15)** underwater where they s __ __ __ __ **(16)** up crabs and fast-swimming fish.

Another creature to watch is the male cormor__ __ __ (17), who dives into the water looking for __ __ __ erials (18) for nest-building.

To catch fresh fish, __ __ __ __ __ ies (19) of herring gulls come to the shoreline. But when they are inland these gulls are s __ __ __ __ ngers (20) and hang out near landf __ __ __ s (21). There are also fish species that feed on __ __ __ __ __ fish (22) and plank __ __ __ (23) at the shoreline.

The Monterey Bay sanctuary is a very valuable center for study and should be pre __ __ __ __ __ d (24) and protected. If you do visit this special museum, you're sure to have a __ __ __ derful (25) time.

Clues

1. Opposite of against
2. Pa's wife
3. Opposite of stand
4. Every
5. Left
6. Organ of smell
7. Pain-in-the-neck kid
8. Soup holder
9. The first number
10. Part of the lower face
11. Artists paint on these
12. Opposite of least
13. Hip-hop music
14. Peril
15. Opposite of short
16. Chicken house
17. Insect
18. Small rug
19. A mark like this :
20. Underground home
21. Sick
22. This goes with peanut butter
23. A heavy weight
24. Start a tennis game
25. Came in first in a race

Answer on page 94.

Spaced Out

What's round and purple and orbits the sun? To find the answer to this riddle, fill in the two blank spaces on each line below to form words that complete the sentences. Then read *down* the column *two letters at a time.*

All space explorations start from   E A R _T_ _H_

The eighth planet from the sun is   N _E_ _P_ T U N E

The water landing of a spacecraft is a   S P _L_ _A_ S H D O W N

The spaceship is driven by a jet   E N G I _N_ _E_

Scientists use telescopes at an   O B S E R V A _T_ _O_ R Y

10, 9, 8, 7, 6, 5, 4, 3, 2, 1 . . .   L I _F_ _T_ O F F

Rockets go into orbit from a   L A U N C _H_ _E_ R

Astronauts measure temperatures in   D E _G_ _R_ E E S

Astronauts ride in the   C _ _ S U L E

On each space trip astronauts do lots of   R _E_ _S_ E A R C H

Answer on page 93.

Creative Cooking

Here's a way to experiment with food in the kitchen. Just add or subtract the indicated letters from the food, rearrange the remaining letters, and make another food or drink that fits the clue in the parentheses ( ).

Example: SHORTBREAD − SHORBR = (fruit from a palm tree) = DATE

1. OATMEAL − O = (hot Mexican food) = *tamale*

2. SANDWICH − WC = (breakfast pastry) = _____

3. PRETZELS − P = (fizzy drink) = _____

4. CUTLET + E = (salad vegetable) = _____

5. RICE + D = (apple drink) = *cider*

6. PESTO + OAT = (round veggies that grow underground) = _____

7. PARSLEY − RLY = (green veggies found in pods) = *peas*

8. PASTRAMI − RIM = (spaghetti, for example) = _____

9. MELON + DEA = (sour drink) = _____

10. PIMENTO − MONT = (popular dessert) = _____

11. SUCCOTASH − SUCSH = (Mexican sandwich) = _____

12. MACARONI − MAAI = (yellow veggie) = *corn*

13. SPARERIBS − SIRB = (green fruits) = *pears*

14. SPINACH − AN = (crispy snacks) = _____

15. TOMATOES − MOE = (breakfast bread) = _____

Answer on page 87.

Healthy Cure

65

Answer each clue and write the answers on the numbered spaces. Then move the numbered letters to the same-numbered spaces in the answer section below. Work back and forth between the clues and the answer section to find out how you can make your own healing concoction.

Clues

A. Polite word __ __ __ __ __ __
50 31 9 53 44 3

B. Breathing organ __ __ __ __
54 49 18 37

C. Hurry __ __ __ __
24 39 2 51

D. Pleasant __ __ __ __
29 55 38 46

E. White crystals that fall from the sky __ __ __ __
12 27 10 20

F. Part of a book __ __ __ __
45 4 14 32

G. Trick or __ (Halloween choice)
__ __ __ __ __
8 16 52 21 40

H. Great __ (large dog) __ __ __ __
19 15 56 33

I. Get older __ __ __
6 57 47

J. The Earth revolves around this
__ __ __
41 1 36

K. Part of a skeleton __ __ __ __
30 43 26 23

L. Took care of a bill __ __ __ __
5 17 35 48

M. Body part at the end of the leg
__ __ __ __
11 25 28 22

N. Tiny particles of dirt __ __ __ __
34 13 7 42

Answer:

__ __ __ __ __ __ __ __ __ __ __ __ __ __ __ __
1 2 3 4 5 6 7 8 9 10 11 12 13 14 15 16

__ __ __ __ __ __ __ __ __ __
17 18 19 20 21 22 23 24 25 26

__ __ __ __ __ __ __ __ __ __ __ __ __ __ __ __ __
27 28 29 30 31 32 33 34 35 36 37 38 39 40 41 42 43

__ __ __ __ __ __ __ __ __ __ __ __ __ __ .
44 45 46 47 48 49 50 51 52 53 54 55 56 57

Answer on page 90.

Scientific Research #2

The name of each scientist in the right column contains a word that fits the clue in the left column. To find this word, cross off some letters in the scientist's name and then read the remaining letters from left to right.

Example: Goal   AIM   A̶SIMO̶V̶

Clue	Answer	Scientist
1. Smart person	_____	BRATTAIN
2. Secret agent	_____	SPERRY
3. Rabbit	_____	HARVEY
4. Price	_____	COUSTEAU
5. Shade of color	_____	HUBBLE
6. Swimming place	_____	LEAKEY
7. Ache	_____	PAULING
8. Face part	_____	CHAPIN
9. Adult male	_____	MARCONI
10. Iced or hot drink	_____	TESLA
11. Veggie on the cob	_____	COPERNICUS
12. Fib	_____	LISTER
13. Squiggly fish	_____	ZEPPELIN
14. Half of twenty	_____	EINSTEIN
15. Measles symptom	_____	ERATOSTHENES
16. Grassy area	_____	LAWRENCE
17. Car fuel	_____	GOETHALS

Answer on page 93.

Found Letters #2

What is a scientific word that means a developmental change in the form of an animal? For the answer to this, find the letter in the word in the right column that is *not* in the word in the left column. Write the extra letter on the blank space. Then read *down* the starred column.

*

RABBLE __ BRAMBLE

THIGH __ EIGHTH

ACORN __ CARTON

SNORE __ REASON

LOSER __ MORSEL

DROVE __ OVERDO

BATHE __ BREATH

STORE __ POSTER

GREAT __ GATHER

GRAND __ DRAGON

CRUEL __ ULCERS

LATER __ RETAIL

REAPS __ SPARSE

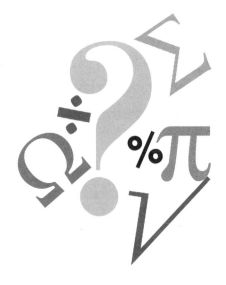

Answer on page 94.

Astronaut's Hangout

Write a letter in the blank space on each line to complete a word or phrase that is meaningful to an astronaut. Then read *down* the starred column to answer this riddle: What is an astronaut's favorite place on a computer?

```
                    *
            AS __ EROID
       BLACK __ OLE
           N __ BULA
      UNIVER __ E
            __ LANET
         GAL __ XY
            __ OMET
        MET __ ORITE

        OR __ IT
         S __ TELLITE
         C __ ATER
```

Answer on page 92.

Intersecting Symbols

In the grid below some letters of the alphabet meet at the intersection of two symbols, one in the Across row and one in the Down column. Example: the letter **A** meets at the intersection of * in the Down column and + in the Across row. Change each intersection point to the letter it represents to read a riddle and its answer. Write the letters on the lines.

	*	!	@	#	$
+	A	D	E	F	H
/	I	L	N	O	P
=	R	S	T	U	W

$= $+   *+   @=   */   !=   @= $+   @+

_____

#+   */   !/   @= $+   */   @+   !=   @=

_____

$=   #/   *=   !+   */   @/   @= $+   @+

_____

$=   #/   *=   !/   !+   ?

_____

$/   #/   !/   !/   #=   @=   */   #/   @/

_____

Answer on page 94.

Creature Body Parts #2

Here's an amazing scientific discovery. You can add the same two letters to partial words to create a creature and a body part. Just take a two-letter piece from the box below and place it in the blank spaces on each line to make the *ending* of a creature's name and the *beginning* of a body part. Write the two words on the lines. We did one for you. Cross off each 2-letter piece as you use it.

BA	CA	CH	~~EA~~	EL
IN	LE	NE	NO	RE
SH	SK	SP	TO	VE

1. F L / **E A** / R S
2. T U R T / __ __ / G
3. A / __ __ / L E E N
4. H A / __ __ / T I N A
5. T H R U / __ __ / O U L D E R
6. M A M / __ __ / C K B O N E
7. O S T R I / __ __ E E K S
8. P O R C U P I / __ __ / R V E S
9. A L P A / __ __ / P I L L A R I E S
10. S Q U I R R / __ __ / B O W
11. M A R L / __ __ / T E S T I N E S
12. P I N / __ __ / N S I L S
13. D O / __ __ / I N
14. R H I / __ __ / S E
15. M O L L U / __ __ / I N

Answer on page 95.

Is There a Doctor in the House?

A two-letter word was removed from each health care worker in the list below and placed in the box. Put each missing piece in the correct blanks to name the worker whose specialty is described in the ( ).

AD	AN	AT	EN	ER
HI	HO	IS	IT	MA
ME	ON	OP	OR	OX

1. P E D I ___ ___ R I C I A N (doctor who takes care of babies and children)
2. ___ ___ T H O P E D I S T (doctor who specializes in skeletal problems)
3. D E R ___ ___ T O L O G I S T (doctor who deals with skin problems)
4. P S Y C ___ ___ A T R I S T (doctor who specializes in mental disorders)
5. O B S T E T R I C I ___ ___ (doctor who delivers babies)
6. N E U R O L O G ___ ___ T (nervous system doctor)
7. P A R A ___ ___ D I C (person who helps doctors give emergency treatment)
8. N U T R ___ ___ I O N I S T (food specialist)
9. S U R G E ___ ___ (doctor who performs operations)
10. C H I R ___ ___ O D I S T (foot specialist)
11. D ___ ___ T I S T (doctor who takes care of teeth)
12. O R T ___ ___ D O N T I S T (doctor who straightens teeth)
13. R ___ ___ I O L O G I S T (x-ray specialist)
14. T ___ ___ I C O L O G I S T (poison specialist)
15. T H ___ ___ A P I S T (person who helps patients recover their physical abilities)

Answer on page 90.

Leather/Middles Weather Riddles

Change the underlined letter in each word to make a new word. If your words are correct you'll find MIDDLES and answers about LEATHER. Write the new words on the lines.

1. WHIT HID SHE DART SOY THEN IS RUINED?

_____

OF THUS SEEPS US, ME FAME IT MAD.

_____

2. THAT TO YON CELL IN WREN IF GAINS THICKENS END

_____

DOCKS? HOWL LEATHER.

_____

3. CHAT DIM TIE FORTH WAND SAT DO SHE MOUTH BIND IT

_____

TOE SMART IF SHE PACE?

_____

OR SOUR PARK, GEL SIT, BROW!

_____

4. WHET DIE ORE RAIL CROP DAY DO THY ETHER GAIN DRIP?

_____

BY PROP AS DIGGER THAT DOUR CLOP.

_____

5. THAT MIND IF STORES GO START BIDS BIKE?

_____

DRAIN STORES.

_____

Answer on page 92.

Number Switch

Replace each numeral with the letter it represents and you'll find an interesting fact about one of the elements. Write the words on the lines.

A = 1   D = 2   E = 3   F = 4

G = 5   H = 6   I = 7   L = 8

M = 9   N = 10   O = 11   R = 12

S = 13   T = 14   U = 15   Y = 16

13 15 8 4 15 12   7 13   4 11 15 10 2   7 10

_____

9 3 1 14 ,   4 7 13 6 ,   1 10 2   3 5 5 13   1 10 2

_____

7 13   10 3 3 2 3 2   4 11 12   6 3 1 8 14 6 16

_____

6 1 7 12   1 10 2   10 1 7 8 13 .

_____

Answer on page 91.

Work Outfits

To find out about some work outfits, change each letter below to the one that comes 2 spaces *after* it in the alphabet. To do this, think of the alphabet as being in a circle and count two letters past the coded letter. For example, **Y** would be changed to **A**. This alphabet circle will help you find the right letters. Write the new words on the lines.

W X Y Z A B C D E F G H I J K L M N O P Q R S T U V (alphabet circle)

BSPGLE Y QNYAC KGQQGML

_____

YQRPMLYSRQ KYW JCYTC RFC

_____

QNYACQFGN. RFGQ QNYACUYJI GQ

_____

AYJJCB CVRPY TCFGASJYP YARGTGRW

_____

(MP CTY). RFC YQRPMLYSRQ UCYP

_____

QNYAC QSGRQ RFYR AMLRPMJ RFCGP

_____

CLTGPMLKCLR QM RFCW FYTC YGP

_____

RM ZPCYRFC, RCKNCPYRSPC AMLRPMJ,

_____

YLB NPCQQSPGXYRGML RM FMJB

_____

RFCGP ZMBGCQ RMECRFCP.

_____

Answer on page 94.

Word Endings

On each line below add a final letter to the given word at the left to make a word described in the parentheses ( ). Then read down the column of added letters to answer this riddle: What do you see in a planetarium?

CHIN ___ (country in Asia)

HAVE ___ (a safe place)

SAG ___ (long story)

MODE ___ (one who poses)

CRAW ___ (move like a baby)

DISCUS ___ (talk)

PRIES ___ (religious leader)

ARE ___ (section)

METE ___ (measuring device)

CARES ___ (stroke)

HEART ___ (fireplace part)

RODE ___ (Western horse event)

VIE ___ (sight)

Answer on page 95.

Body-Part Creatures

You've already learned how to make creature body parts. Now you can make body-part creatures. Just take a two-letter piece from the box below and place it in the blank spaces on each line to make the *ending* of a body part and the *beginning* of a creature. Cross off each 2-letter piece as you use it.

AD	CH	EA	EE	ER	LE	LL
LY	NE	PE	SH	ST	TA	TH

1. W A I / __ __ / O R K
2. G A L L   B L A D D / __ __ / M I N E
3. A O R / __ __ / N A G E R
4. B O / __ __ / W F O U N D L A N D
5. H E / __ __ / D E R
6. B E L / __ __ / N X
7. K N / __ __ / L
8. C O R N / __ __ / G L E
9. E Y E L A / __ __ / A R K
10. M U S C / __ __ / M M I N G
11. S T O M A / __ __ / H U A H U A
12. S K U / __ __ / A M A
13. W I N D P I / __ __ / N G U I N
14. M O U / __ __ / R U S H

Answer on page 94.

77 Habitat for a Scientist

All living things need a habitat, or special place, of their own. Some of the habitats studied by scientists are scattered below. Put them in alphabetical order into the grid and then read *down* the starred column. You'll find the first and last names of a famous marine biologist and writer.

ZONE

COPSE

WOODS

LAB

AVIARY

JUNGLE

STEPPE

PASTURE

HATCHERY

ORCHARD

ARBORETUM

PRAIRIE

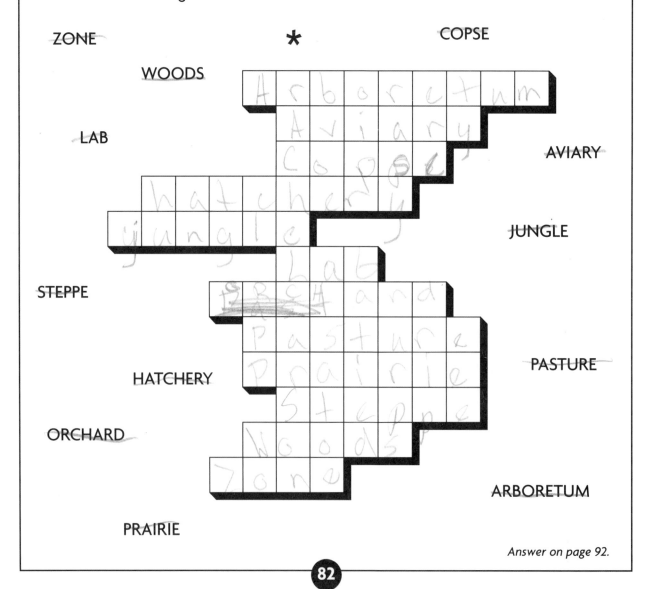

Answer on page 92.

Uh-Oh!

Write a letter in the blank space on each line to spell something that can cause a lot of sorrow and suffering. Then read *down* the starred column to find out what these events are called.

```
                    *
          T O R    __    A D O
      B L I Z Z    __    R D
    W I N D S      __    O R M
            H      __    R R I C A N E
          E A      __    T H Q U A K E
            G      __    L E
            F      __    O O D

                   __    E L U G E
          W H      __    R L W I N D
          T W I    __    T E R
          S Q U    __    L L
      T E M P E    __    T
                   __    Y P H O O N
    C Y C L O N    __
                   __    I P T I D E
        L A N D    __    L I D E
```

Answer on page 95.

Mini Fill-Ins #3

Complete each grid by putting the words into the spaces where they belong.

Elements

ARGON   OXYGEN
ARSENIC   TIN
CESIUM   XENON
HELIUM   ZINC

National Parks

ACADIA
ARCHES
HALEAKALA
OLYMPIC
YELLOWSTONE
YOSEMITE
ZION

Water Places

AQUEDUCT
CANAL
FJORD
INLET
RESERVOIR
STRAIT
TRENCH

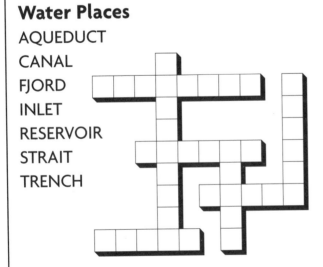

Dangerous Sea Critters

ANEMONE   SEA SNAKE
BARRACUDA   SHARK
CORAL   SQUID
MORAY EEL

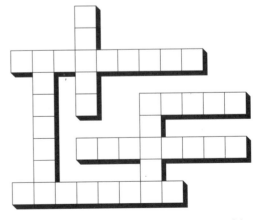

Answer on page 94.

Scrambled Creatures

Each word in the list has been scrambled and made into a new word before it was put into the grid. So, **RAT** is in the list but **ART** is in the grid. To find all these *scrambled* words, look across, up, down, and diagonally, both forward and backward. Circle each word when you find it. When you have all the words circled, write the *leftover* letters from the grid on the spaces below. Keep the letters in order, from left to right and top to bottom, and you'll find what these scrambled words are called.

1. CAT
2. RAT
3. TUNA
4. SABLE
5. ADDER
6. EGRET
7. HARE
8. RAIL
9. FLEA
10. SOLE
11. VOLE
12. OWL
13. APE
14. SPIDER
15. MARE
16. TERN
17. SARDINE
18. HORSE
19. SNAKE
20. WASP
21. ANT
22. HORNET
23. NEWT

```
T  E  E  R  G  W  K  R  A
C  H  N  T  O  P  A  E  S
A  L  R  L  D  R  E  A  D
U  A  E  O  A  I  N  M  G
N  I  N  S  N  D  S  R  A
T  R  T  E  I  E  M  F  N
B  A  L  E  S  S  W  A  P
S  E  R  W  E  N  T  E  E
S  H  O  R  E  V  O  L  A
```

Hidden answer: _ _ _ _ _ _ _ _ _ _

Answer on page 95.

Our Precious World

Figure out the word or phrase that completes each sentence and find it in the same-numbered row in the diagram. Cross out the answer, letter by letter. All the letters of an answer will always be next to each other, but there will be extra letters on each line. When you are finished, write these *leftover* letters in the blanks in position at the bottom of the page. Work from left to right and top to bottom, and you'll find an important message.

1. Disposal areas for garbage are called ___.
2. Animals or plants that no longer exist are ___.
2. Some chemicals are poisonous, or ___.
3. Dense tropical areas are called ___ ___.
4. The part of the atmosphere that blocks out the sun's harmful rays is the ___ ___.
5. Coal and oil formed by the remains of ancient life are called ___ ___.
6. Species that are in peril of dying out completely are ___.
7. A dry area like the Sahara is a ___.
7. The skeletal material that makes up a reef is called ___.
8. The oldest U.S. national park is ___.
9. The gradual increase of the earth's temperature is called global ___.

1	P	R	L	A	N	D	F	I	L	L	S	O	T
2	E	X	T	I	N	C	T	E	T	O	X	I	C
3	R	A	I	N	F	O	R	E	S	T	S	C	T
4	T	H	O	Z	O	N	E	L	A	Y	E	R	E
5	E	F	O	S	S	I	L	F	U	E	L	S	A
6	R	E	N	D	A	N	G	E	R	E	D	T	H
7	S	D	E	S	E	R	T	R	C	O	R	A	L
8	Y	E	L	L	O	W	S	T	O	N	E	E	S
9	W	A	R	M	I	N	G	O	W	A	T	E	R
10	U	U	L	T	R	A	V	I	O	L	E	T	R
11	E	R	O	S	I	O	N	C	S	O	L	A	R
12	E	S	S	O	L	I	D	W	A	S	T	E	S

9. The liquid needed for plant and animal life is ___.
10. The rays of the sun that cannot be seen are ___ rays.
11. The wearing away of soil or rock is called ___.
11. The use of the sun to heat a house is known as ___ energy.
12. Some of the materials in sewers are called ___ ___.

Hidden message: __ __ __ __ __ __ __   __ __ __   __ __ __ __ __ __ ' __

__ __ __ __ __ __ __ __ __ __

Answer on page 94.

Answers

1. A to Z

Examine	Ask
Query	Observe
Demand	Scrutinize
Discover	Explain
Investigate	Inquire
Search	Determine
Seek	Probe
Quiz	Judge
Inspect	Figure out
Try	Prove
Sample	Verify
Recogni ze	Unearth
Study	Review

8. Location, Location

P A R A S I T E
1 2 3 4 5 6 7 8

Answer: parasite

15. Going Batty

1. Acrobat
2. Batches
3. Bathrobe
4. Batman
5. Baton
6. Batter
7. Battery
8. Battle
9. Battleship
10. Debate
11. Incubator
12. Sunbathers
13. Rebate
14. Sabbath

17. Intersecting Numbers

What do you get if you cross a kangaroo and a raccoon? A fur coat with pockets.

25. Filling Station #1

1, 2, 3, 4, 5 = Utter
6, 7, 8, 9 = Lies
10, 11, 12 = Red
13, 14, 15, 16 = Rent
17, 18, 19, 20 = Foot
21, 22, 23 = Hit
24, 25, 26, 27 = Wash
28, 29, 30 = Ear
31, 32, 33, 34, 35 = Right
36, 37, 38, 39 = Core
40, 41, 42 = Dad
43, 44, 45 = Tea
46, 47, 48 = Cub
49, 50, 51 = Sat
52, 53, 54 = Hen
55, 56, 57 = Fir
58, 59, 60 = Ten

Butterflies are different from moths in two ways. They are brightly colored and they have clubs at the end of their antennae.

31. General Science

1. Insecticide	11. Bacteria
2. Tornado	12. Sodium chloride
3. Decompose	13. Hurricane
4. Shivering	14. Hydroponics
5. Microbes	15. Atmosphere
6. Microscope	16. Precipitation
7. Cerebellum	17. Molecules
8. Evaporate	18. Sandblasting
9. Hypothesis	19. Smallpox
10. Experiment	20. Nutrients

38. Material Things

```
      S T R I N G
      P A P E R
P L A S T I C
B A T T E R Y
          C A N
      B O T T L E
M A G A Z I N E
```

Answer: Recycle

42. Found Letters #1

River	A	Arrive
Mailed	C	Decimal
Agent	L	Tangle
Blend	O	Blonde
Grates	N	Strange
Snail	E	Aliens
Drapes	S	Spreads
Peril	T	Triple
Hotel	A	Loathe
Shape	R	Phrase
Trait	S	Artist
Mares	T	Stream
Taller	A	Lateral
Veins	T	Invest
Trace	E	Create

Answer: A clone star state

47. Ear-ing Aid

1. Appearance	9. Nearest
2. Beard	10. Pearls
3. Clearing	11. Rehearsal
4. Early	12. Researcher
5. Earnest	13. Shear
6. Earrings	14. Spear
7. Earthquake	15. Swear
8. Earthworm	16. Tearing

53. Letter Switch

Riddle: What is the best way to catch a squirrel?
Answer: Climb up a tree and act like a nut.

64. Creative Cooking

1. Tamale	9. Lemonade
2. Danish	10. Pie
3. Seltzer	11. Taco
4. Lettuce	12. Corn
5. Cider	13. Pears
6. Potatoes	14. Chips
7. Peas	15. Toast
8. Pasta	

2. Criss-Crossing Trees

9. The Machine Age

Jackhamm **e** r
Ha **r** vester
G enerator
Bulld **o** zer
Turbi **n** e
Co **p** ier
Co **m** pressor
Typewr **i** ter
C omputer
Fac **s** imile

Answer: Ergonomics

20. Backing In

1. Amary**lli**s
2. A**nem**one
3. **But**tercup
4. Car**nat**ion
5. Clema**tis**
6. Daffo**dil**
7. **Gar**denia
8. Im**pat**ience
9. **I**ris
10. Laven**der**
11. **Mari**gold
12. **May**flower
13. **Nar**cissus
14. Periwin**kle**
15. Pe**tun**ia
16. **Pop**py
17. **Snap**dragon
18. **Snow**ball
19. Sw**eet** William
20. Wist**eria**

26. 1-2-3

Why is a thermometer the most educated thing in a lab?
It has so many degrees.

32. Food Experiments

1. Marry
2. Shift
3. Leave
4. Beagles
5. Planet
6. Robin
7. Roses
8. Pearls
9. Lilacs
10. Groan
11. Ancient
12. Print
13. Upset
14. Smile
15. Croak
16. Lakers
17. Noon
18. React
19. Chews
20. Crowd

43. Inside Outer Space

1. THERE ARE SEVEN USED CARS IN THE DRIVEWAY.
2. WHO WANTS A TURNOVER FOR DESSERT?
3. DID YOU HEAR THAT JOKE ABOUT THE CLOWN?
4. PLEASE COME TO MY PARTY.
5. WE'LL VISIT THE ALAMO ON FRIDAY.
6. TIME TO WORK ON YOUR GRAMMAR, SON.
7. HE'S AN INEPT, UNEDUCATED RAT!
8. THE STATION IS JUST AROUND THE CORNER.
9. AL PACINO VACATIONED THERE.
10. THIS UNUSUAL PAINTING IS ON SALE.
11. THE PLANE TAXIED DOWN THE RUNWAY.

49. Seeing Stars

Answer: Astronomer

52. Mini Fill-Ins #2

Herbs   **Jeweler's Materials**

Weather   **Tree Parts**

54. Close Relatives #2

1. Face Parts
Jaw
Mouth
Cheek
Lips

2. Flowers
Daisy
Rose
Sweet pea
Lily of the valley

3. Trees
Weeping willow
Date palm
Cherry
Pine

4. Fruits
Grape
Plum
Peach
Apple

5. Deer
Fawn
Stag
Moose
Elk

6. Horses
Pony
Stallion
Colt
Mare

7. Leg Parts
Ankle
Knee
Foot
Shin

8. Arm Parts
Wrist
Hand
Finger
Funny Bone

9. Meats
Pork
Steak
Veal
Lamb

10. Vegetables
Peas
Lima beans
String beans
Squash

11. Seasons
Summer
Winter
Fall
Spring

12. Body Organs
Liver
Lungs
Heart
Brain

3. Coded Riddle

Where do Martians leave their spaceships? At parking meteors.

10. For the Birds

Riddle answer: A pool pigeon.

16. Cross-Offs

a. mole, mouse, rat
b. wan, woven, win, when
c. Uranus, Pluto, Venus
d. liver, steak, veal, pork
e. babies, toddlers
f. panther, tiger, zebra, lion
g. silver, bronze, gold
h. care, acre, race
i. macaroni, ziti, spaghetti
j. tomorrow, yesterday, today
k. lagoon, pond, sea, lake

Answer: They get wrinkled and turn
   into raisins.

27. Elementary Fun

1. **Bar**ium
2. **Car**bon
3. **Cob**alt
4. **Cop**per
5. **Gold**
6. Io**dine**
7. Kryp**ton**
8. **Lith**ium
9. **Man**ganese
10. Mer**cury**
11. **Ne**on
12. **Nit**rogen
13. Pla**tin**um
14. **Pot**assium
15. **Sod**ium
16. Sul**fur**
17. **Tit**anium
18. Tungs**ten**
19. U**ran**ium
20. Zir**con**ium

33. Problem Solving

1. L A C K O F   F O O D
2. L B C K O F   F O O D
3. L B C K A T O O D
4. L B C K A T I O D
5. L B R K A T I O D
6. L B R N A T I O D
7. B R N A T I O D
8. B R N A T I O N
9. B E R N A T I O N
10. H I B E R N A T I O N

Some animals (like bears) can't get enough food in the winter so they hibernate.

39. Circulation Fact

A. Nursery
B. Salad
C. Mine
D. Noon
E. Wiggle
F. Task
G. Heals
H. Exact
I. Loose
J. Binds
K. Batty
L. Attend
M. Wart

Answer: Blood brings oxygen and nutrients to the cells and takes away waste materials.

44. Same Starts #1

1. Venom
   Venus
   Venison
2. Potassium
   Potato
   Potent
3. Metabolism
   Metric
   Method
4. Cancer
   Cannibal
   Canyon
5. Gall bladder
   Gallon
   Galapagos
6. Calcium
   Calories
   Callus
7. Heron
   Herring
   Heredity
8. Everest
   Everglades
   Evergreen
9. Petrified
   Petroleum
   Petri dish
10. Cobalt
    Cobweb
    Cobra
11. Chimpanzee
    Chipmunk
    Chicken pox
12. Starfish
    Starch
    Stamina

48. Filling Station #2

1, 2, 3, 4 = Corn
5, 6, 7, 8 = Hemp
9, 10, 11, 12 = Rate
13, 14, 15, 16 = Each
17, 18, 19 = Nun
20, 21, 22 = Red
23, 24, 25, 26 = Dirt
27, 28, 29 = Fog
30, 31, 32 = Son
33, 34, 35 = Let
36, 37 = In
38, 39, 40 = Tee
41, 42, 43, 44 = Hand
45, 46, 47 = The

In California the temperature reached one hundred and thirty-four degrees on July tenth nineteen hundred and thirteen.

56. Criss-Crossing Fish

61. Squish Squash

1. Lettuce/cabbage
2. Belly/abdomen
3. Helium/radon
4. Condors/wolves
5. Measles/mumps
6. Taste/touch
7. Zinc/nickel
8. Siamese/Persian
9. Meadow/pasture
10. Gorilla/gibbon
11. Mercury/Jupiter
12. Hydrogen/oxygen
13. Pacific/Indian
14. Constrictor/python
15. Lens/pupil
16. Starch/sugar
17. Tangerine/cantaloupe
18. Pistachio/filbert

4. Science Study

1. Bio**log**y
2. Electromag**net**ism
3. **Cry**ogenics
4. **Dend**rology
5. Cli**mat**ology
6. **Tax**idermy
7. Me**tall**urgy
8. **Arch**aeology
9. **Rob**otics
10. **Astro**nomy
11. Her**pet**ology
12. Ana**tom**y
13. Bo**tan**y
14. **Met**eorology
15. **Zoo**logy

22. Scrambled Fact

Birds only sleep in nests when they are having babies. At other times they sleep any place. They can doze on tree branches; they can sleep while standing at the beach or when they are flying. They are able to do this because one half of their brain sleeps and the other half is awake.

28. Hot Stuff

1. Water	5. Sand
1. Arid	6. Dunes
2. Oasis	6. Mesas
2. Nomad	7. Flash flood
3. Cactus	8. Windstorms
3. Root	9. Camels
4. Scorching	9. Gobi
5. Lizard	

Answer: Death Valley (California)

40. Criss-Crossing Body Parts

```
S T O M A C H   T O N S I L S
H       P         O O       P
O     S P L E E N   S H     I
U       E   Y       G E     N
L E G   N   E       U   K N E E
D       D     H E A D   D
E   W A I S T       O
R       X   H   T R A C H E A   D
        O   T       E       E   N
    F I N G E R     A       A   O
        A   A R M   E A R   R   I
B R A I N   X             T     D
O       L       L I V E R       O
N               I               I
E L B O W       P A N C R E A S
```

45. Throw It Out!

The following are crossed out (in order):

Orange rind	Moldy cheese
Chicken bone	Eggshell
Banana peel	Fish bone
Apple core	Potato skin
Peach pit	Clamshell
Stale bread	Grape seed

Grid answer: Microbes crumble food into tiny bits. (Under grid: These bits then turn into gas, a process called decomposition, or simply rotting.)

50. Some Fisherman!

PIKE
CARP
SHARK
STURGEON
WHITING
ANCHO**VY**
HADD**OCK**
SALM**O**N
TR**OU**T
POR**GY**
HAL**I**BUT
BA**SS**
TUNA

Answer: Ichthyologist

55. Create-a-Creature

1. Hamster	13. Boar
2. Leopard	14. Tiger
3. Mink	15. Toad
4. Viper	16. Porpoise
5. Beaver	17. Eagle
6. Ermine	18. Pelican
7. Shrew	19. Raven
8. Turtle	20. Boxer
9. Camel	21. Spaniel
10. Swine	22. Cricket
11. Shark	23. Moth
12. Weasel	24. Zebra

58. Center Line

Ans **w** ers
Shr **i** vel
Bli **s** ter
Pal **e** tte
Knu **c** kle
Imp **r** ove
Fan **a** tic
Tea **c** her
Man **k** ind
Pea **s** ant

Answer: Wisecracks

Eme **r** ald
Dep **o** sit
Wel **c** ome
Boo **k** let

Hat **c** het
Adv **a** nce
Gra **n** ite
San **d** bar
Cop **y** cat

Answer: Rock candy

65. Healthy Cure

A. Please	H. Dane
B. Lung	I. Age
C. Rush	J. Sun
D. Nice	K. Bone
E. Snow	L. Paid
F. Page	M. Foot
G. Treat	N. Dust

Answer: Use a paste of sugar and water on nonbleeding cuts to speed up healing.

71. Is There a Doctor in the House?

1. Pediatrician	9. Surg**eon**
2. **Orth**opedist	10. Chiropodist
3. Dermatologist	11. **Dent**ist
4. Psych**iat**rist	12. Ortho**dont**ist
5. Obstetric**ian**	13. **Radi**ologist
6. Neuro**log**ist	14. **Tox**icologist
7. Para**medi**c	15. **Ther**apist
8. Nutr**iti**onist	

5. Transplanted Body Parts

1. C
2. E
3. G
4. F
5. I
6. M
7. K
8. J
9. L
10. H
11. D
12. A
13. B

11. Close Relatives #1

1. **Dogs**
   Fox terrier
   Great Dane
   French poodle

2. **Insects**
   Yellow jacket
   Roach
   Water bug

3. **Fish**
   Brook trout
   Sting ray
   Black sea bass

4. **Amphibians**
   Frog
   Toad
   Newt

5. **Healthy Foods**
   Oat bran
   Whole wheat bread
   Skim milk

6. **Junk Foods**
   Cream puff
   Candy
   French fries

7. **Mammals**
   Wild goat
   Polar bear
   Blue fox

8. **Baby Animals**
   Chick
   Calf
   Foal

9. **Forest Workers**
   Park ranger
   Logger
   Wood chopper

10. **Plant Parts**
    Stem
    Leaf
    Root

11. **Birds**
    Dove
    Hawk
    Parrot

12. **Precipitation**
    Sleet
    Snow
    Hail

13. **Metals**
    Gold
    Silver
    Copper

14. **Snakes**
    Adder
    Viper
    Rattler

34. Read It!

S aga
S **c** ript
Thr **i** ller
E pic
Roma **n** ce
Ane **c** dote
R **e** port

F able
Memo **i** r
Comi **c** s
T ale
D **i** ary
N **o** vel
Yar **n**

Answer: Science fiction

46. 5s, 6s, 7s, 8s

TO **P** AZ
US **H** ER
KA **Y** AK
ON **S** ET
SK **I** MP
P **R** OVE
HE **L** LO
C **L** OWN
OU **G** HT
MA **Y** BE

Science: Physiology—the study of the functions and activities of living organisms

PLA **S** MA
SCRO **L** L
CAT **C** HY
SQU **I** NT
ROBO **T** S
VAL **L** EY
CHRO **M** E
BEG **G** AR
CRA **Y** ON

Science: Sociology—the study of society and social groups

EXH **A** UST
PAR **S** LEY
INS **T** EAD
QUAR **T** ER
CABO **O** SE
RES **P** ECT
ARC **H** ERY
ACR **Y** LIC
BLO **S** SOM
DEL **I** GHT
CRA **C** KLE
MES **S** AGE

Science: Astrophysics—the study of celestial objects and phenomena

ADOP **T** ION
AQUA **R** IUM
WETL **A** NDS
SCH **E** DULE
PANO **R** AMA
TRA **N** SMIT
FAI **T** HFUL
PALO **M** INO
DWEL **L** ING
THE **O** RIES
GARG **O** YLE
PLA **Y** TIME

Science: Paleontology—the study of past geological periods from their fossils

73. Number Switch

Sulfur is found in meat, fish, and eggs and is needed for healthy hair and nails.

6. Constellation Find

1. **And**romeda
2. **Boo**tes
3. Camelo**par**dalis
4. **Can**cer
5. **Cap**ricorn
6. **Car**ina
7. **Cham**aeleon
8. **Crat**er
9. **Gem**ini
10. **Men**sa
11. Micros**cop**ium
12. Oc**tan**s
13. Pega**sus**
14. **Pho**enix
15. **Sag**ittarius
16. Ser**pens**

12. Eye Cue

CELL	**O**	PEN
TRAM	**P**	RICE
PLUS	**H**	AIR
CHAR	**T**	RAIL
FORT	**H**	ILL
SAG	**A**	WAKE
EASE	**L**	ADDER
SPAS	**M**	OTHER
RODE	**O**	WING
GAVE	**L**	EVER
PINT	**O**	PAL
THIN	**G**	HOST
SWAM	**I**	CON
DISCUS	**S**	PRINT
FINES	**T**	RAVEL

Answer: Ophthalmologist

18. Eensy-Weensy

Di**mi**nutive
Tiny
Minus**cul**e
Mini**atur**e
Suba**to**mic
Itty-**bit**ty
Littl**e**
Small

Answer: Microbes

29. Criss-Crossing Mammals

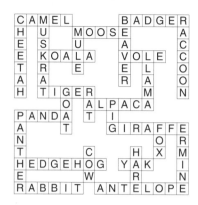

36. Opposite Distraction

1. **Arm**strong
2. Dar**win**
3. **Die**sel
4. **Far**aday
5. **Hall**ey
6. **Her**schel
7. **Low**ell
8. Max**well**
9. Men**del**
10. **New**ton
11. **Past**eur
12. Ruther**ford**
13. De**war**
14. Wr**ight**

61. Simile Scramble

1. Happy as a lark
2. Mad as a hornet
3. Blind as a bat
4. Hungry as a bear
5. Sly as a fox
6. Red as a lobster
7. Loose as a goose
8. Eager as a beaver
9. Slow as a snail
10. Gentle as a lamb
11. Bold as a lion
12. Crazy as a loon
13. Wise as an owl
14. Proud as a peacock
15. Quiet as a mouse
16. Fat as a pig
17. Bald as an eagle
18. Stubborn as a mule
19. Weak as a kitten
20. Busy as a bee

69. Astronaut's Hangout

AS **T** EROID
BLACK **H** OLE
N **E** BULA

UNIVER **S** E
   P LANET
GAL **A** XY
   C OMET
MET **E** ORITE

OR **B** IT
S **A** TELLITE
C **R** ATER

Answer: The space bar

73. Leather/Middles Weather Riddles

1. What did the dirt say when it rained? If this keeps up, my name is mud.
2. What do you call it when it rains chickens and ducks? Fowl weather.
3. What did the north wind say to the south wind at the start of the race? On your mark, get set, blow!
4. What did one rain drop say to the other rain drop? My plop is bigger than your plop.
5. What kind of storms do smart kids like? Brain storms.

78. Habitat for a Scientist

Answer: Rachel Carson (author of "The Sea Around Us" and "Silent Spring")

7. Mini Fill-Ins #1

Fowl

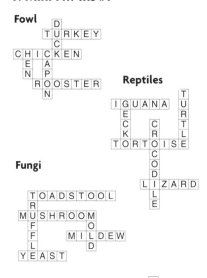

```
        D
  T U R K E Y
        C
C H I C K E N
E       A
N       P
  R O O S T E R
        N
```

Reptiles

```
              T
              U
I G U A N A   R
  E       C   T
  C       R   L
  K   T O R T O I S E
          O   E
          D
    L I Z A R D
          I   E
          L
          E
```

Fungi

```
T O A D S T O O L
R
M U S H R O O M
F           O
F     M I L D E W
L           D
Y E A S T
```

Cattle

```
      D
      O
      G   H
  B O V I N E
  U     E I
  L       F
C A L F   S T E E R
O           R
W
```

13. Cute Critter

A water bear is a tiny creature no bigger than one grain of sand. When it cannot find water it stops eating, moving, and breathing, and seems to be dead. But when scientists add water to it, the tiny animal comes back to life.

21. Name Dropping

Famous scientist: Louis Pasteur

23. Creature Words

1. Top
2. Bag
3. Boat
4. Cot
5. Lean
6. Lead
7. Hate
8. Jar
9. Sew
10. Tie
11. West
12. Maze
13. Grill
14. Son
15. Feet
16. Crib
17. Rider
18. Dark

30. Scientist's Snack

Fudge
Cookie
Pastry
Sherbet
Brownie
Popcorn
Candy
Cake
Doughnut
Licorice
Pretzel
Biscuit

Riddle answer: Fission chips

35. Job Search

```
P B O M O C S C T T
* L A B O R A T O R Y
  A S J N G T A L U P
  N S E T A N R L M I
* T E C H N I C I A N
  S T T S S P H E N G
```

Answer: Laboratory technician

51. Creature Body Parts #1

1. Locust / stomach
2. Jaguar / arms
3. Giraffe / feet
4. Crab / abdomen
5. Turkey / eyebrow
6. Whale / legs
7. Swan / ankle
8. Sardine / neck
9. Finch / chin
10. Wasp / spine
11. Iguana / navel
12. Moth / thigh
13. Mosquito / toes
14. Termite / teeth
15. Toad / adenoids

57. Stormy Scientists

Riddle Answer: They blast off.

59. Same Starts #2

1. Protoplasm
   Proton
   Protozoa
   Protein

2. Coma
   Compass
   Computer
   Compound

3. Salk
   Salamander
   Salmon
   Saliva

4. Spacecraft
   Spasm
   Spaniel
   Sparrow

5. Carbon
   Cardiologist
   Caribou
   Carrier

6. Mandarin
   Mango
   Manganese
   Manatee

7. Spider
   Spinach
   Spine
   Spitz

8. Cheetah
   Chemistry
   Checkup
   Chemotherapy

9. Species
   Spectrum
   Spearmint
   Spelunker

10. Parka
    Parsley
    Parsnip
    Partridge

11. Barnacle
    Barometer
    Barley
    Bark

12. Forecast
    Forest
    Formula
    Fortify

63. Spaced Out

Ear **th**
N **ep** tune
Sp **l a** shdown
Engi **ne**
Observa **to** ry
Li **f t** off
Launc **he** r
De **gr** ees
C **ap** sule
R **es** earch

Answer: The planet of the grapes

66. Scientific Research #2

1. Brain
2. Spy
3. Hare
4. Cost
5. Hue
6. Lake
7. Pain
8. Chin
9. Man
10. Tea
11. Corn
12. Lie
13. Eel
14. Ten
15. Rash
16. Lawn
17. Gas

19. Bug Off!

Riddle answer: He is bright for his age.

14. Cold Stuff

1. Ice	5. Floes
1. Freezer	6. South Pole
2. Penguins	7. Whales
3. Glacier	7. Krill
3. Snow	8. Crevasses
4. Alaska	9. Satellites
4. Alps	10. Blue
5. Seals	10. Blubber

Answer: Continent of Antarctica

24. Bright Beginnings

Learn	Rare
Avenue	Ebony
Black	They
Oscar	Renter
Regret	Ideal
Alike	Event
This	Valley
Olive	Emerge
Remote	Reach
Yearly	Sketch

Answer: Laboratory Retrievers

41. Scientific Research #1

1. Bunk	10. Rest
2. Pole	11. Rot
3. Cave	12. Chick
4. Pie	13. Red
5. Doe	14. Lad
6. Fan	15. Key
7. Gale	16. Chart
8. Cell	17. Bus
9. Cure	

62. Museum Guide

1. Cali**forni**a	14. En**danger**ed
2. **Mar**ine	15. A**long**
3. Vis**itor**s	16. **Scoop**
4. B**each**es	17. Cormor**ant**
5. **Twenty**-six	18. **Mat**erials
6. Bottle**nose**	19. **Coloni**es
7. Inverte**brates**	20. **Scav**engers
8. **Can**yon	21. Land**fills**
9. Abal**one**	22. **Jelly**fish
10. Ur**chins**	23. Plank**ton**
11. W**easels**	24. Pre**serve**d
12. Al**most**	25. **Won**derful
13. Tr**app**ers	

67. Found Letters #2

Rabble	M	Bramble
Thigh	E	Eighth
Acorn	T	Carton
Snore	A	Reason
Loser	M	Morsel
Drove	O	Overdo
Bathe	R	Breath
Store	P	Poster
Great	H	Gather
Grand	O	Dragon
Cruel	S	Ulcers
Later	I	Retail
Reaps	S	Sparse

Answer: Metamorphosis

69. Intersecting Symbols

What is the filthiest word in the world? Pollution.

74. Work Outfits

During a space mission astronauts may leave the spaceship. This space-walk is called Extra Vehicular Activity (or EVA). The astronauts wear space suits that control their environment so they have air to breathe, temperature control, and pressurization to hold their bodies together.

76. Body-Part Creatures

1. Waist / stork
2. Gall bladder / ermine
3. Aorta / tanager
4. Bone / newfoundland (dog)
5. Head / adder
6. Belly / lynx
7. Knee / eel
8. Cornea / eagle
9. Eyelash / shark
10. Muscle / lemming
11. Stomach / chihuahua
12. Skull / llama
13. Windpipe / penguin
14. Mouth / thrush

79. Mini Fill-Ins #3

Elements

National Parks

Water Places

Dangerous Sea Critters

81. Our Precious World

1. Landfills	7. Coral
2. Extinct	8. Yellowstone
2. Toxic	9. Warming
3. Rain forests	9. Water
4. Ozone layer	10. Ultraviolet
5. Fossil fuels	11. Erosion
6. Endangered	11. Solar
7. Desert	12. Solid wastes

Answer: Protect the earth's resources.

37. Lost Letters

1. Stale	B
2. Bacon	E
3. Faulty	C
4. Border	A
5. Dress	U
6. Thirty	S
7. Father	E
8. Surgeon	T
9. Peasant	H
10. Fasts	E
11. Trout	Y
12. Claps	M
13. Spot	U
14. Compete	L
15. Moral	T
16. Maze	I
17. Insect	P
18. Fight	L
19. Fling	Y
20. Timer	B
21. Reading	Y
23. Copes	I
22. Power	D
24. Sole	V
25. Wring	I
26. Mined	D
27. Phones	I
28. Metal	N
29. Bride	G

Riddle

```
S P E A S A N T S T R S T
U R E W O P L C N G C T H
R B R K L D R E S S O S A
G P E B E L S S P H M A I
E N M N Z S E N O H P F F
O G I Q B T Z T X E A L
N M T R E A D I N G T U I
M A Z E W L C M M H E L N
B R I D E E O O E V Q T G
T H I R T Y P R N T Z Y R
L T U O R T E V C L A P S
N M Y B W X S M O R A L Z
```

answer: Because they multiply by dividing.

71. Creature Body Parts #2

1. Flea/ ears
2. Turtle/ leg
3. Asp / spleen
4. Hare / retina
5. Thrush / shoulder
6. Mamba / backbone
7. Ostrich / cheeks
8. Porcupine / nerves
9. Alpaca / capillaries
10. Squirrel / elbow
11. Marlin / intestines
12. Pinto / tonsils
13. Dove / vein
14. Rhino / nose
15. Mollusk / skin

75. Word Endings

Chin**a**
Have**n**

Sag**a**
Mode**l**
Craw**l**

Discus**s**
Pries**t**
Are**a**
Mete**r**

Cares**s**
Heart**h**
Rode**o**
Vie**w**

Riddle answer: An all-star show

78. Uh-Oh!

tor **n** ado   **d** eluge
blizz **a** rd   wh **i** rlwind
winds **t** orm   twi **s** ter
h **u** rricane   squ **a** ll
ea **r** thquake   tempe **s** t
g **a** le   **t** yphoon
f **l** ood   cyclon **e**
      r iptide
land **s** lide

Answer: Natural disasters

80. Scrambled Creatures

1. Act	13. Pea
2. Art	14. Prides
3. Aunt	15. Ream
4. Bales	16. Rent
5. Dread	17. Sandier
6. Greet	18. Shore
7. Hear	19. Sneak
8. Lair	20. Swap
9. Leaf	21. Tan
10. Lose	22. Throne
11. Love	23. Went
12. Low	

```
T E E R G W K R A
C H N T O P A E S
A L R L D R E A D
U A E O A I N M G
N I N S N D S R A
T R T E I E M F N
B A L E S S W A P
S E R W E N T E E
S H O R E V O L A
```

Hidden answer: Anagrams

Index

Index key: (puzzle number), puzzle page, **answer page**.